Misfit Magic School

MARINA J. BOWMAN

For all who have some misfit magic in them.

This is a work of fiction. Names, characters, places, and incidents either are the product of the author's imagination or are used fictitiously. Any resemblance to actual persons, living or dead, events, or locales is entirely coincidental.

Copyright © 2022 by Code Pineapple

All rights reserved. No part of this book may be reproduced or used in any manner without written permission of the copyright owner except for the use of quotations in a book review.

First paperback edition September 2022

Written by Marina J. Bowman

ISBN 978-1-950341-77-1 (hardback)

ISBN 978-1-950341-76-4 (paperback)

ISBN 978-1-950341-78-8 (ebook)

Published by Code Pineapple

www.codepineapple.com

CONTENTS

1. The Test of Age — 1
2. Glofiara — 12
3. Girl on Fire — 19
4. Initiation — 25
5. Facing Magical History — 34
6. A White Lie — 45
7. Open Heart — 55
8. Secret Keeper — 63
9. A Pixie's Vision — 69
10. The Five Eyes — 75
11. Revenge — 84
12. A Pesky Dotted Chimera — 94
13. The Menagerie — 103
14. Wild Goose Chase — 111
15. The Witness — 117
16. The Whispering Woods — 123
17. The Gatekeeper — 128

18.	The Zookeeper	143
19.	Traces and Sigils	150
20.	The Spy	157
21.	Fallen Heroes	162
22.	A Ghostly Specter	171
23.	Something to Hide	179
24.	Dogamar Duty	187
25.	A Cloaked Figure	194
26.	Shape-Shifter	201
27.	Betrayed	207
28.	The Golden Invitation	221
About the Author		232
Endnotes		

Chapter One

THE TEST OF AGE

Ember Pearson was having a bad day. No, scratch that, she was having a bad week. Horrendous, if she was using the adjective correctly. She had been learning about them at school—the normal human one—just last week when her parents announced out of nowhere that she was taking her test of age that Sunday.

Of course, she had been training for it pretty much her entire life, so it should have been easy. Except, Ember had almost burned down the ceremony hall.

The car jolted as it hit a particularly bad pothole. Ember's elder sister, Summer, nudged her with her shoulder. "Wake up, sleepyhead. We're almost there."

Ember yawned and straightened her spine. They had been traveling for over ten hours. She hadn't been sleeping, not really, but she didn't want to wake up to the nightmare of her new life. Like her sister, and her parents before them, Ember had dreamed of going to Zanith, School of Arcane. It had been her dream even before she understood what magic really meant.

And then, she had ruined her demonstration and had been labeled a remnant, a misfit in the magical society. There was only one place for misfits like her.

"I don't see it," Ember said, squinting at the dark, looming trees ahead.

"Glofiara is hidden by a powerful enchantment that turns the forest sentient and gives it powers of the sentry," Ember's mother explained. "You can't see the school unless the veil falls so that the humans can't accidentally trespass."

"But it goes both ways, right?" Ember countered. "So it's basically a prison." Humans were not the only ones being kept out; the remnants were being kept in. It couldn't be more obvious to Ember.

"Only to protect you," Ember's father said. Ember gritted her teeth in an attempt not to scream. She didn't need to be saved, but her family had started to look at her differently since she had failed her test of age. They looked at her like she was a ticking time bomb and they couldn't wait to get rid of her. Her father had brought the silk gloves that she was expected to wear everywhere. And, literally, the very next day after the ceremony, they had started calling people, pulling strings, and doing whatever was necessary to get her the first seat in Glofiara.

"That's a lot of security for children," Ember muttered.

"Remnants," Summer corrected her. "Historically, they have been the ones who have caused the most disasters and accidents, by a large margin, almost exposing us to the human world." Remnants, aka people who couldn't properly channel ether, the source of magic.

Her parents' faces tightened. Summer had said the unspoken out loud. It didn't matter how her parents or sister tried to spin things—*it'll be good for you, blah, blah, blah*- Ember saw Glofiara for what it truly was: a place to send away hopeless children, or, as they were more popularly called, remnants.

Ember made a face. "What about Mallorus, the evilest black sorcerer in history? He's not a remnant." Ember knew she had said the wrong thing, because the atmosphere in the car turned almost chilly.

"Let's not talk about him now," her mom said. Ember's parents had both been part of the group of powerful white sorcerers that had defeated Mallorus twenty years ago, but a lot seemed to have changed since then.

"Fine," Ember said, folding her arms over her chest. "Just admit that non-remnants have done equal harm to society. What about the thief you were chasing last month—the one who could change faces? He was a full-fledged sorcerer, wasn't he?"

"I don't know why you're being so difficult. Glofiara isn't a punishment," Summer said snootily. "At the school, the remnants are taught to get their powers under control and—" Ember blocked out the rest of her sister's lecture. Her words sounded rote, taken right off the pamphlet of Glofiara that her dad had brought home.

"It just sounds like a long detention to me," Ember said. Until she'd turned thirteen a few months ago, she had seen the way her parents tiptoed around her whenever she was unable to summon a flame or summoned too much of it. Never on her will, as if her magic had a mind of its own. They just didn't have a name for her until she actually failed the test put forth by the Ether Conservation Society that chose the path of a young magic user.

Her dad chuckled. "I assure you that's not the case. You have many things to learn there, and besides, I know of many people who graduated and went on to become esteemed members of society."

"And how many of them were warlocks, let alone sorcerers?" Ember countered.

"No job is big or small," her mom reminded her. "An office clerk is as important as a warlock!"

Ember grumbled under her breath. That might as well be true, but a desk job lacked the excitement that a sorcerer or even a low-level witch profession would bring. She had seen her parents go off on adventures, often as long as a few months. They would seek impenetrable treasure beneath the ocean, chart a course through the world to seek an elusive but notorious smuggler, or stop a disaster from happening in the first place and save the world.

Ember's parents were heroes, not only hers but of the entire magical community. They were revered and respected amongst all, and their glory had only grown since their encounter with Mallorus.

Ember wanted the same excitement. She wanted to feel the wind in her hair, salt on her tongue, and fresh snow in her hands when she was on an important mission. But she couldn't do that stuck at Glofiara. Ember calculated the years ahead of her glumly. While people who had passed the test would train to become a fledgling witch, she would spend the next seven years trying to become something she wasn't—at best, a boring clerk at the Society headquarters, or at worst, a networker in the human world who reported potential magic threats. Either way, Ember wouldn't be a part of any of the cool stuff.

"How do we get inside?" Summer asked, craning her head out of the car to take a better look at the vast, impenetrable forest.

"We're supposed to be here by noon," Ember's dad said. "And the school will let us inside."

Summer checked her watch. "Looks like we are three minutes early."

As if on cue, there was a low, dull groan, and the forest cleared a wide path ahead to let them inside. The tendrils seemed to stretch towards them almost ominously as the car rolled into the forest. Glofiara Academy for Remnants and Non-Magics loomed in the distance. It was perched on the arms of a small hillock while the rest of the forest spread below.

Ember held in a breath until they climbed the slope to the feet of the school. The Pearson family wasn't the only one there. The courtyard was full of cars, chariots, and other means of colorful transport. Even more were arriving behind them. There must have been at least forty different families. Even though there were many magical schools spread out on different continents, there was only one for remnants.

"That's a lot of remnants," Ember's father remarked under his breath.

"More than last year?" Summer asked. Like Ember and their father, she had flaming red hair that glistened under the afternoon sun. Ember hated her hair. It reminded her of the fire that she couldn't tame.

As soon as Ember and her family walked out of their car, they were surrounded by people. They had questions, so many questions about her parents' presence at Glofiara, and about Ember, who had become a point of discussion in every magical household, or so she assumed. After all, how could the progeny of the legendary George and Rosetta Pearson turn out to be a remnant?

Ember had never felt so isolated from her family in her entire life. She shuffled her feet and walked ahead, almost bumping into someone. "I'm sorry," she said, looking up to find a brown-haired girl with glasses juggling a non-magic gadget. Ember had nearly knocked the video recorder out of her hands. "Great, already causing trouble, Ember," she mumbled to herself.

"Isn't that why we are all here?" a voice said. A lanky boy with dirty-blond hair was smirking at her. Her gaze dropped to his left arm, which was missing a hand. She knew that he had observed the burn scars that crisscrossed down her arms. Even though they had faded and turned white over time, they were still noticeable.

"And you are?" Ember asked.

"Parker," he said, walking up to her. He had a cocky swagger about him that reminded Ember of the kids at her human school. Ember didn't like him right away. Something about him spelled trouble, and she knew she ought to steer clear of all of that, especially if she wanted to get into Zanith. Ember didn't plan on sticking around for too long.

This was a conversation she'd had with her sister Summer last week. Ember had been whining about going to Glofiara when Summer had let her in on a lesser-known fact that changed Ember's mind. Some rare kids could upgrade themselves from a remnant to a full-fledged ether user and even transfer to Zanith, provided their behavior was excellent and they learned to get their powers under control. She just had to be patient about it.

"I wasn't expecting to run into a Pearson here," another voice said. A new boy walked into their circle. His voice had a faintly Middle Eastern accent. He had swarthy brown skin and a head full of curls. Like the girl Ember had bumped into, he wore glasses, but they were of a more stylish design.

"I'm Elias Kamali," he said. "Nice to make your acquaintance, Miss Pearson. I've heard splendid things about your kin."

"Well, my kin is right there," Ember said, pointing at her parents and sister, who didn't seem to realize that she was no longer with them. They were talking to the other parents gathered around them—or, more likely, adoring fans.

"The tales of your family's bravery and courage have reached every corner of the world, including my small town. I'm pleasantly surprised to run into you here."

Ember stopped herself from rolling her eyes. Elias was a Pearson fanboy.

"Nobody speaks like that anymore, dude," Parker said, scoffing.

Elias frowned at him. "I was just trying to be polite."

"Is this guy for real?" Parker asked, pointing his thumb at Elias. "And what's with the snooty accent?"

Elias's frown deepened. "I'm not in a state to deal with an ignorant fool."

Parker's jaw dropped open. "Did you just—"

Parker was interrupted by a thundering voice. It seemed to come out of everywhere, yet Ember couldn't spot the speaker. "Attention, prospective students of Glofiara. We welcome you to a new term."

"Who is talking?" Parker asked, looking around in confusion.

Elias frowned. He seemed to do that a lot. "This wasn't mentioned in the manual."

"You read the manual?" Parker said. Under his breath, he added, "Nerd."

"I heard that," Elias said.

"I meant you to."

"Oh, give it a rest, will you?" Ember said.

"Ah, that's Headmistress Kinnera," Elias said, gesturing at someone in the distance.

Ember raised her head just as a podium seemed to rise out of nowhere whilst the headmistress floated in midair before stepping down. Ember realized that Headmistress Kinnera was a physical warlock, or maybe even a sorcerer.

"She's definitely dramatic," Parker observed.

Ember nodded. Magic in their world was made of four parts: elemental, like Ember's fire; physical, like the power of invisibility; natural, like the power of plant manipulation; and spirit, like the ability to read minds. There was a fifth kind—the dark kind—but no white sorcerers or warlocks talked about it.

Headmistress Kinnera tapped on the mic thrice. "My dear children," she said, her gaze sweeping over the crowd. It lingered on her longer than necessary. "I welcome you to your first term at the Glofiara School for Remnants and Non-Magics."

After the brief introduction by Headmistress Kinnera, the parents said goodbye to their children. Ember's mother sniffed as she hugged her. "This is very hard for me."

"You're leaving me here by your own choice," Ember said. "I didn't ask for this." It was true that remnants had very limited options, unlike a fledgling witch. Besides Glofiara, her only other option was to be homeschooled. "You can teach me better than anybody else here."

"Ember—" Rosetta Pearson began. "You know I would if I could—" Ember heard the truth fill up the gaps. *We already tried and don't have the time for you.*

"You're abandoning me," Ember said desperately.

"You'll be safer here with people who are like you," her mother continued. "We don't have enough experience with, well…" She drifted off.

"That's what you think," Ember replied tartly.

Ember's father frowned at her, adjusting his glasses on the bridge of the blunt nose that Ember had inherited from him. "Come now, don't speak to your mother in that manner."

A twinge of guilt twisted her stomach. She had never been away from home. Her parents usually brought her and Summer on their adventures, wherever they went. She had spent a good number of years in the non-magic world, living amongst humans. And when the time had finally come to take her rightful place among fledgling witches, just like Summer, she had been ousted. The fact that Summer had gotten an internship at the Conservation Society right after her graduation didn't help things either. Ember had always felt isolated in her family. While Summer had excelled at her powers, Ember could never sustain a proper flame no matter how hard she tried. Deep down, she'd known she was a remnant long before she had failed the test. And now more than ever, she felt the distance between them widening like a chasm.

"Rosetta, George," said a voice behind them. Ember turned. Headmistress Kinnera was walking towards them. She was much taller than either of Ember's parents, with a willowy frame. She wore a red mantle, like every member of the Society who passed the test of age. She had a shrewd look, and something about her made Ember distrust her right away. "I see you've brought your youngest along. Never thought I would see you here."

Ember thought it sounded like a snub.

George nodded, good-natured as ever. "She's your responsibility now."

"Of course," Kinnera said. "I take care of every child as my own."

Ember was pretty sure that she had seen the headmistress make a girl with pigtails cry just a few moments prior. Everything about her was polished, from her long flowy dress that didn't have a single wrinkle to her shiny black boots.

Ember looked down at her own shoes. They were coated with mud.

"Do you hear that, Ember?" Rosetta said. "We have known Kinnera for years. She's going to take good care of you."

"Yes," Kinnera said, peering down at Ember. "Nothing gets past me, ever." It sounded like a threat, and Ember had a feeling that the headmistress didn't like her.

"And this must be your elder daughter," Kinnera said, turning her owlish gaze to Ember's older sister, who in turn gave her a charming smile.

George nodded, looking at her proudly. Ember had never seen him look at her that way. "She just earned a coveted spot at the Society as an initiating warlock."

Both of Kinnera's brows rose. "That's impressive. But I expect nothing less from a daughter of the Pearson family." She glanced down at Ember briefly as if to let her know that she was the exception.

Ember hugged her arms to her chest while scowling. She didn't need the reminder.

Rosetta checked her pocket watch. "Oh, dear, we are running late. I'm afraid we have a train to catch, and humans are surprisingly efficient with the schedules."

Kinnera nodded. "Of course." Around them, parents were saying goodbye to their children. Elias and his parents were in some discussion, while Parker was hugging his mother. The girl with the video recorder stood to the side alone, shuffling her feet.

Ember's parents kissed her goodbye. Her dad leaned in and said, "I know you're angry at us, but trust me, this is for your own good."

Ember nodded. She would combust if she heard that line again.

"Promise you'll write to us when we're in Peru," Mom said. "And that you'll call us. You have that brand-new communication device in your bag." Unlike normal humans, the magic society didn't come up with fancy names for its equipment. They were the same as the name suggested. Ember had always found this difference amusing.

"I will," Ember said, tears gathering in the corners of her eyes.

Even Summer looked a little teary when she hugged her. "And promise me you will behave," she said.

"Okay," Ember said, looking up at the hulking building that stretched above them. It wasn't too fancy, nor too shabby. Glofiara was just itself—prim, proper, and lacking any proper adventure. Or so Ember reasoned. There was nothing awe-inducing about it, no grandeur, unlike the opulence of Zanith that seemed to burst at its seams with magic. Compared to that, Glofiara was rather unremarkable.

"Remember that is the only way to—"

"—get to Zanith," Ember finished. "Yeah, I know."

Headmistress Kinnera frowned as if she had overheard their conversation. Ember watched her family get into their dented Corvette and drive away. Almost immediately, the headmistress's entire demeanor seemed to change.

She stared down at Ember icily. "I have dealt with my fair share of remnants," the headmistress said. "And I know a troublemaker when I see one."

Before Ember could say anything, the headmistress turned on her heels and vanished into thin air. Parker was right. She had a flair for dramatics.

Ember picked up her carry-on and followed her classmates past the tall wrought-iron gate. As the last student entered, the gate closed with an ominous groan, and as the last parent was swallowed by the forest, the trees went back to their original position, forming an impenetrable wall of darkness once again.

Chapter Two

GLOFIARA

Ember dragged her suitcase to the feet of the dark and hulking building that seemed to have weathered with time, tiny cracks appearing all over and moss clinging to its walls. It had four spiraling towers at the top that stretched as far as the eye could see. There was something crooked about it, and ancient. Three tall white columns were embedded at the top of the steps that led to the vast, oak door. As Ember climbed the steps, her eyes scanned the symbols etched into them.

The front doors opened into a vast foyer with a large marble statue in the middle. It was of a woman in a top hat, wearing flowy clothes with small children standing close to her. They were all staring up at the sky. "Magic is boundless, and so are you," the caption below read.

"That's Leighton Aeger," Elias said when he caught Ember staring. "She was the founder of Glofiara, about a hundred years ago. She wanted to build a sanctuary for remnants when they were deemed society outcasts."

"Looks like nothing has changed in the last hundred years then," Ember muttered under her breath. Her parents had been quick to wash their hands of her and drive away with the perfect daughter.

Elias raised a brow. "I'm sensing some kind of tension here."

"You a clairvoyant?" Ember countered, folding her arms in front of her chest.

Elias immediately stiffened and walked away without saying another word.

"Weirdo," Ember muttered under her breath. She had no idea what was up with him.

The new students were clustering together, chatting and laughing in small groups. Ember had no intention of being in a clique, or making friends for that matter. She wasn't planning on staying here for long, and they might distract her from her goals.

As if Parker had somehow read her mind, he appeared beside her. "Do you know any people around here?"

"Not particularly," Ember said. She recognized a few faces from the times her parents had dragged her to parties. There was no one as famous as she was, and Ember was aware of the gazes that trailed after her as she walked up to the giant bulletin board where she hoped to get her bearings.

"I get the feeling you are not much of a talker," Parker said.

And you talk way too much, Ember thought to herself.

Ember walked up to the lady sitting next to the bulletin board. She handed over a small brown envelope to her.

"What's this?" Ember asked curiously.

"Your welcome packet. It has your class schedule. The book list has been mailed to your parents. Or you can make a payment to the school office yourself, if you desire."

"I'll make it myself," Ember said, producing a checkbook that her parents had given her on her tenth birthday. They might not have time for her, but they had all the money in the world. Ember knew that her parents wouldn't have time to write a check when they were battling giant carnivorous plants or whatever they were doing in Peru.

Both Ember and her sister had been managing their expenses since they were very young. That was why they had the weirdest things at their home—like an enchanted trombone, a talking toad that could repeat everything you said in short croaks, and a self-writing quill, amongst other things. Their parents never seemed to notice.

"Thank you," the lady at the desk said. She was very wrinkly, like she was a hundred years old. She produced a key and a talisman locket.

Ember stared at the talisman. "What is this?"

"The talisman must be worn at all times at school by remnants and non-magics. No exceptions," she said. "There will be orientation dinner at night. Attendance is mandatory. First-year rooms are in the North Tower. Your roommate has been pre-assigned." She sounded like a machine.

"Thanks," Ember muttered, dragging her suitcase to the stone staircase that led upstairs. She hoped that she was taking the right path. Above her, enchanted letters flying in the air spelled "East Tower."

Ember grunted under her breath in frustration as she trudged downstairs before finding her way up to the North Tower. By the time she reached upstairs, she was already panting. Her room was on the fourth level of the tower. She opened the door with her feet, tripped, and fell flat on her face.

There was an excited squeal, and Ember thought for a second that she had walked into an aviary. A mousy, brown-haired girl stood over her. She was the same girl from outside that Ember had noticed before, the one with the video-recorder. She was gazing at her almost owlishly.

"Are you my roommate?" the girl asked breathlessly.

"Appears so," Ember said, sitting up.

"Hi, I'm Chloe. Chloe Queen," she said, blushing a little as if her name embarrassed her.

"And I am—"

"You're a Pearson," the girl breathed in awe. "I've read your parents' autobiography cover to cover."

Ember stifled a groan. "Yes, I am." Ember's parents had published many books over the years, but any about Mallorus were glaringly absent, almost as if they liked to pretend that he simply didn't exist.

"Wow," the girl said, her large glasses fogging. "It's truly an honor."

Ember cocked her head at the girl. "Why? I think you're confusing me for my parents." Ember didn't mean to be rude, but she was tired of people acting like she meant something because of her parents.

"Weren't you the one who solved the crime of stolen goblin gold last month?" the girl asked.

Ember sighed. "No, that would be my older sister, Summer. I'm the useless younger remnant sister, Ember."

The girl's cheeks colored, and she looked away. "I don't think you're useless."

Ember shrugged. "Maybe, but I'm definitely the dangerous one."

Chloe frowned at her. "Anyway, why are you so late?"

"I lost my way, and the suitcase took me hours to bring up," Ember said.

"The school is enchanted," Chloe said. "If you talk nicely to the walls, they even get your suitcase up for you."

As Ember watched, she walked to the wall and tapped on one of the bricks thrice. Almost immediately, the bricks began to shake and quiver all the way down to where her suitcase lay on the ground. The bricks laid it in the space under one of the two canopy beds. "Would have been nice to know before," Ember muttered.

"I know a few people who studied here before me," Chloe said.

Ember nodded. Chloe carrying around the human device made more sense now. Most of the remnants graduated out of Glofiara and assimilated themselves with the human society.

Ember sat down on her bed and started to unpack her rucksack. The contents spilled over as soon as she sat it down on the bed, and out jumped a gigantic toad.

Chloe gasped and took a step back. "That's a…"

"Toad," Ember said, wincing. Her roommate was not supposed to see him, at least not so soon. She'd had every intention of keeping him hidden away when she had sneaked him out of the house with her.

"Toad, toad, toad," it repeated. It croaked like any other frog, but the sounds it made sounded eerily like actual words.

"Oh my Ethilenne, did it just say toad?" Chloe said. "It can talk?"

"Talk, talk, talk," it repeated.

"This is my pet toad, Toasty," Ember said, sounding a little defensive. She scooped the fat toad in her hands, and it leaped up to her shoulders where it sat, croaking.

Chloe was still in shock, her hands cupping her cheek. "I've never met a talking toad before."

"Toasty is a failed experiment. He was enchanted by an evil sorcerer using toadstools to terrorize villages in rural Belarus," Ember said, petting the toad, which had an unusually warm belly.

"So that story is true then?" Chloe said. "Your parents defeated him, didn't they?"

Ember nodded. "Yes, but he was nowhere near as evil or powerful as Mallorus."

Chloe flinched. "Yikes!"

Ember rolled her eyes. "It's not like he can jump me from behind the curtains. He's locked away in Tellarus." Nobody had ever escaped Tellarus. It was no ordinary prison but an enchanted one. It housed the most dangerous and notorious warlocks, but it had no guards. Instead, Tellarus was locked away in a space-time dimension that was inaccessible to everyone except those in charge at the Ether Conservation Society.

But Ember could understand Chloe's wariness. Mallorus had wreaked havoc on the magical community in the three years when he had come to power. He was an empath and had the rare ability to manipulate people's emotions to do his bidding. He had been a charming candidate for the Conservation Society elections about twenty-five years ago, and people had been enthralled by him until he was found to have murdered his opponent, who was the then-Chancellor of the Society.

After that, Mallorus didn't bother hiding his true identity. Overnight, he seemed to have amassed followers who believed what he had to say. He created a new organization called the Order of Shadows to oppose the Society's reign, and killed important political and religious figures in the magic world. Even the remnants weren't spared. All around the world, remnants began disappearing from their human society posts. The Conservation Society did what they could to protect the magical community, but everything Mallorus did was unpredictable chaos. He was unstoppable.

That was when the white sorcerers, a.k.a. Ember's parents and a few others from the Society, were called in to stand against him. He had terrorized the magic world and the humans' for three years before he was finally banished.

"You are the daughter of Pearsons; you're so fearless, just like they are," Chloe said in awe. "I'm so glad that we can be friends."

At the mention of the word "friends," Ember said, "Listen, Chloe, I think you are great, but I don't really do friends."

"What do you mean?" Chloe asked. She cocked her head to the side.

"No offense to you, but I don't plan on staying here for a long time."

"You mean you're going to escape?" she asked.

"No," Ember said, shaking her head. "I'm going to Zanith and—" she started to say but then thought better of herself. She didn't have to tell Chloe about her plans. "That's all you need to know."

Chloe's back hunched as she made her way to her bed. Ember tried not to feel bad about it. Besides, she was just setting up boundaries and trying not to get attached, because Chloe obviously wore her heart on her sleeve. She would be heartbroken when Ember eventually left.

Ember pulled out her notebook and cracked her knuckles. She had a game plan. She and Summer had come up with it together.

1. *Keep my head down and stay out of any drama.*

2. *Be on my best behavior and follow all the rules.*

3. *Convince the teachers AND my parents that sending me here was a mistake.*

4. *Get into Zanith.*

5. *Become a sorcerer and go on epic adventures like my parents.*

For the first time in several weeks, Ember was actually feeling optimistic.

Chapter Three

GIRL ON FIRE

Ember examined the parchment paper that had her timetable. She scanned through her classes. She had at least five each day, except on weekends. They had classes for Arithmetic, Science, Facing History, Natural Care of Plants and Animals, Cartography, Book Planning, Historical Myths and Confluence of Magic, and even something called Creativity, amongst others.

"What is this?" she muttered to herself. There were no classes for technique or channeling, no classes for controlling the unstable source of magic housed by the remnants. Summer had told her all about life at Zanith and how exciting it was. All the students entered as fledgling witches, or Witchies, as popularly called, and were already asked to tackle various "projects" that would prepare them for real-world problems. Meanwhile, Ember was stuck taking classes with no apparent practical knowledge. How lame was that! This was no different than the human school that her parents enrolled her in whenever they had to go on an adventure and couldn't leave Ember alone.

Ember wasn't expecting Zanith-level magic-attunement, but this was abysmal. She stared down at her schedule, but nothing changed.

Evening was falling rapidly outside the window. Ember stood there, watching the sprawling forest beneath. It was spread over acres and acres of land, as far as the eye could see, with an impenetrable denseness.

"We should get ready for dinner," Chloe said, not quite meeting Ember's eyes. She had changed into an oversized lavender sweater with patchwork. Even though it was barely autumn, a chill climbed up Ember's spine.

"Sure," Ember said. The awkwardness was so thick between them, Ember could practically cut it with a knife. "Listen, Chloe—"

"It's fine," she said. "You don't have to be my friend if you don't want that. I know I'm not exactly popular with people."

Ember sighed. "You have to understand that it's not about you."

"It's you," Chloe said. "Gotcha." Her gaze lingered on Ember's arms. She must have caught sight of the faint scars when she was changing into her denim jacket. Ember always preferred wearing full-sleeved clothes when she was out, and she never really had to share a room with someone who wasn't her sister.

Toasty the toad croaked loudly, catching their attention. The sound appeared to be a cross between "me" and "go," maybe both. Ember sighed and kneeled beside him on the bed. "You can't go anywhere out of this room, understand? I don't think we are allowed to have pets."

"We aren't," Chloe confirmed.

Ember sighed. "You can't leave this room. Do you understand? Or you'll have to go live with Summer." Both Toasty and Ember knew that Summer didn't care much for amphibians, especially a fat toad with a penchant for eating doughnuts. "Good boy." She put out a small bowl of nuts and crickets—Toasty's favorite food. Chloe made a face at the sight of the insects.

"I pegged Toasty for a girl," Chloe said as they left the room. Ember was relieved that Chloe seemed to be coming out of her shell. She felt bad for icing her out when she'd offered her hand in friendship.

The other first-year girls were coming down the stairs. They seemed to have worn their finest for the first night feast. Ember looked down at her own faded jeans and ratty sneakers. Two snooty-looking girls walked past them wearing identical expressions of disgust, as if they thought Ember and Chloe had crawled out of a sewer.

They made their way downstairs. Thankfully, the enchanted signs still floated above them, telling them exactly where they needed to go. Chloe had her weird little machine out, and she was recording everything.

"Are you sure that's allowed?" Ember asked.

"I was thinking of making a vlog about our experiences and uploading it on MagicNet. There isn't much information about Glofiara online, and I'm sure the prospective students will find everything helpful!"

Ember wasn't convinced. "There's a reason Glofiara isn't popular. I don't think anybody is here by their own choice. People don't exactly look forward to being remnants." A.k.a. the outcasts, uncontrollable freaks in the magical community.

"I guess," Chloe said. Ember's words didn't seem to deter her, however, as she continued descending the stairs while shooting. Ember walked ahead of her, trying to memorize the vast hallways that seemed to stretch for an eternity. She figured that the North and East towers were for students while the West and South ones were for the teaching staff. The classes, meanwhile, were held in the inner sanctum.

"Fun fact about Glofiara: it was originally built to be a temple before the plan was scrapped, and decades later the first headmistress Leighton Aeger took over." Chloe continued talking to the camera.

That would explain the wonky architecture, Ember thought to herself. The shimmering signs pointed them to the main quad, which opened up to a large amphitheater that resembled the sitting area of the Colosseum, with the seats made of polished granite instead of rough sandstone. It had floor-to-ceiling windows that let light in, and the center held a large banner that had the school emblem with a raised platform in the middle.

"What is that you're always carrying around, weirdo?" said a voice behind Ember. She recognized it as the short, blond-haired girl that she had noticed in the courtyard. She wasn't alone. She had three more people behind her, and Parker was one of them. Ember was amazed by how quickly they had formed a clique, but bullies had a way of gravitating towards each other. Ember was surprised that Parker was one of them. She had pegged him to be the harmless, class-clown sort.

"This is my video-recorder," came Chloe's indignant voice.

Ember tried to ignore the rest of the conversation and walked ahead. This was not her problem to deal with.

"No way, creep," the girl's high-pitched voice said. "Are you recording us?"

"No, I wasn't," Chloe said, sounding dismayed. "You're not even in the video."

There was a sound of dull rattling, and then Chloe's soft sob. "Stop, you'll break it."

"We mean no harm," came another voice, snickering this time. Ember stopped walking.

"Please give my video-recorder back," Chloe cried.

"We will, once we inspect the footage," came a taunting reply.

Ember couldn't ignore it anymore. She turned on her heels and exited the hall. Just outside, the four classmates gathered around Chloe. Parker held the video-recorder in his good hand while he poked the screen with a finger. "How do you even work these human gadgets?"

Chloe tried to reach for it, but Parker, who was a good five inches taller than her, held it out of her grip.

"She told you to give it back," Ember said, hands on her hips. All five of them turned to face her.

"What are you, her mother?" snorted one of the girls, flipping her hair.

"Yeah, seriously, stay out of it," another said.

"Give. Her. The. Recorder. Back," Ember said, enunciating each word.

"Or else?" the blond girl challenged. She took the video-recorder from Parker and threw it on the ground.

Parker stared at her in surprise while she smirked. "What did you do that for, Clarisse? That's rude."

Clarisse didn't react. "Oh, grow a backbone, Parker."

Ember didn't think; she reacted. Twin flames erupted down the length of her arms, but they didn't burn or sear her skin. The fire was a part of her, just as she was a part of it.

"Firestarter," screamed one of the children, their mocking smiles replaced by a look of horror in an instant. Fire was the rarest of the five elemental powers, and the most dangerous one. Fire-users had a destructive reputation.

"Don't worry," Clarisse said. "It's not like she will hurt us."

"Yeah, we meant no harm," Parker said, looking nonplussed. He looked like he wanted to defuse the situation, which made Ember even angrier. They were the ones who started it.

"She can't scare us," Clarisse said, raising her own hands. "We're not afraid to use our powers either."

"Really?" Ember said. "Try me." A faint buzzing sound took over her ears, which usually indicated that the fire was about to spread more than just down her arms. That had happened to her during the exhibition of the test of age, where she had lost control and almost burned the entire hall down.

She took another few steps, and the children scattered. "This isn't over," Parker said, taking two steps back. Ember basked in the aftermath of her victory until she realized that the fire wouldn't go out. She tried flapping her arms, but small flakes of ember floated down to the ground. She had only meant to scare off the bullies, without thinking of the aftermath.

"You're on fire," Chloe said, her eyes wide in awe and fear.

Chapter Four

INITIATION

E mber winced. She had forgotten what came afterwards.

There were rapid footsteps behind her. A woman wearing half-moon spectacles and a flowing maroon mantle appeared around the corner. "Why is everybody crowding the hallway?"

The woman gasped when she saw Ember standing in the middle of the corridor with her arms stretched out like a scarecrow, quite literally on fire. With a sinking feeling, Ember realized that she was already messing up her strategy for getting out of this place.

"What is the meaning of this?" the older woman asked.

Ember was at a loss for words, but a younger woman with deep brown skin rushed past the first lady. Both of them were dressed in the same colored mantle, which indicated that she was a teacher at Glofiara, as well.

"Allow me," she said, a kind smile on her face.

Something about her put Ember at ease almost immediately. She walked right up to her—not caring about the flames that crackled on her arms—brushed a hand down to the back of her head, and pressed lightly. Almost immediately, the flames died down.

Ember gasped. "You're a conduit." A powerful one at that. It had taken at least three of them at the Conservation Society to douse her flames during the test.

"I am," the woman replied. Her tight curls were pulled up into space buns. She was wearing a moon-print shirt tucked into corduroy pants paired with giant black boots. She was probably the prettiest person Ember had ever seen. "My name is Nadine, but people just call me Nadie. What's yours?"

"Ember," she replied, blushing deeply.

"I'm glad you're safe, Ember," Nadie said. With a wink, she added, "How ironic is your name?"

Ember was glad that Nadie could joke, especially in a situation like this when Ember knew she was in deep trouble. The other woman hurried up to them with a dark scowl on her face. "What is the meaning of this, Professor Owsmann?"

"She's safe now, Irene," Nadie replied. "That's what's important."

"Safe?" Irene replied. "She put the students around her in grave danger. This could have led to an even bigger fire!"

"Relax, everything's fine. She's safe."

"She's the last person I'm worried about," Irene said, glaring at Ember, who stared back obstinately. "I'm the school mother. It's my job to take care of my students," Irene said. She reminded Ember of one of the strict nuns that she had met when she went to a Catholic school last fall.

"If you took better care of them, you would know that one of them was being bullied," Ember retorted stonily.

Irene was furious. Nadie glanced worriedly between Ember and the older women before she turned to the former. "Is it true? Were you protecting another student?"

"It doesn't matter what she was doing," Irene said. "She's supposed to be wearing the warding talisman at all times on the school grounds. She used her powers without authorization or school permit, something first-years are forbidden to do."

Ember blanched. So that was what the talisman was for. Just like Nadie, it was a conduit of sorts.

"I have to report this to the headmistress," Irene said. "This calls for detention."

"It's fine, Mother Irene," Nadie said, glancing at Ember once. "I'll deal with her."

Irene observed Nadie warily. "Are you sure?"

"You're the one who gave me responsibility as the school guardian for the first-years," Nadie kindly but firmly reminded the other woman.

"I gave it to you because I wanted you to learn—" She glanced at the students around them. "Well, never mind." And then more softly, "They're here for a reason, you know?"

Ember's ears burned at this subtle remark. She knew exactly what Mother Irene meant. She had heard of a similar concept in the human world, a place where all the naughty children went when they were out of control. This place might be nice to look at, but it was still a prison.

"Thank you, Irene," Nadie said. She nodded at the other woman, who gave Ember one last withering look before she walked to a group of students and shepherded them inside the Main Hall.

The commotion had attracted quite a few curious spectators. Elias was one of them. Her ears throbbed at the attention.

"I'm sorry," Ember began. "They were bullying my roommate, and I couldn't just watch them do it."

"So you reacted in the worst possible way and let your powers control you," Nadie said. Unlike Irene, she didn't look angry, just faintly disappointed. Ember didn't know why that bothered her. She didn't even know the woman.

Ember shook her head. Unwittingly, she had already found trouble, something she desperately wanted to avoid. "That wasn't my intention." But she was a remnant. There was a reason she hadn't been initiated as a fledgling witch. Her powers were unstable and chaotic, and nothing good ever came of them, something that everyone around her seemed to remind her of every waking second.

"Save it," Nadie said. "I don't want to do it, but I unfortunately have to punish you."

Ember's heart sank. She'd thought Nadie was different, but she was just like the other teachers.

"Come by my office tomorrow after you're done with your classes," she said. She had a thick accent and spoke with a slight drawl to her words.

"Yes, ma'am," Ember said.

"And, Ember?" Nadie said, turning around to face her again. "Wear that talisman around your neck. It's supposed to be worn all the time."

Ember fished out the talisman, feeling the weight of it rest just below her collarbone. She felt no different, but she knew the talisman was there to rein in her powers. Meanwhile, the crowd had started to disperse.

Chloe walked up to her, not quite meeting her eyes. "I'm sorry that happened to you because of me."

Ember shook her head. She was angry at Chloe, as well. "It's not my job, or anybody else's, to defend you. Why didn't you use your powers? The more you let people walk all over you, the more they will take advantage of you."

She started to turn away when Chloe's voice came from behind, so quiet that she wasn't sure she even heard her at first. "I don't have any powers."

Ember whirled around. "What do you mean you don't have powers?"

The light from the electric sconces above them reflected on her face. "It's Glofiara School for Remnants and Non-Magics, remember? I'm the latter," Chloe said in a flat tone.

Ember bit her tongue. She had never met a non-magic before. It was rare to not have powers passed down through your family, like remnants. It was considered especially unlucky not to have any powers at all. According to the first verse of magic, ether was all-permeating, present all around.

Le Domina de Fiara etherene, all magic starts and ends with ether. Ember had heard that all her life.

If there was someone who had it even worse than remnants, it was non-magics like Chloe.

"I'm sorry," Ember said, shuffling her feet awkwardly.

"Why?" Chloe said. "I like you because you don't pity me. It's either that or people finding ways to take advantage of me. It isn't easy being the weakest one in the room." Chloe spoke as if today's incident wasn't an isolated one.

"Is your human gadget okay?" said a voice. Elias hovered in front of them. He was still wearing all black clothes, kind of like her parents' vampire friends from Romania.

Chloe turned the video-recorder in her hand. "The screen is a little cracked, but the lens seems fine."

"Why do you carry that around, anyway? Don't you have a comm-device?" Elias asked.

"I do, but I like this one better," Chloe said, clutching the battered video-cam to her chest. It obviously had some sort of a sentimental value to her.

Elias nodded. "Well, you better hurry inside lest someone catches you here. The Initiation is about to begin, and especially after what happened, you don't want to be in trouble so soon."

Ember scowled at his high-and-mighty tone. She pushed past him and took a seat on one of the empty rows at the top. Chloe hovered around the door before taking a seat on the other side of the Main Hall. Ember didn't know why that bothered her. Her plan was to maintain her distance.

A few moments passed before a loud bang echoed through the hall. The dais that had been empty just a few moments prior began to fill with teachers as they emerged out of a thick cloud of smoke. All the teachers wore the maroon mantle with the crest of the school sewn into it. Ember spotted Nadie at one end of the line. There were ten of them apart from her.

A tall man with wire-framed glasses and an argyle sweater kept staring at Nadie, or maybe calling her Professor Owsmann was more appropriate. When she turned to face him, he appeared almost star-struck. Somebody seemed to have a little crush. Ember's eyes flitted on each of the teachers, stopping momentarily over the tall man with a tattooed face that disappeared inside the robe he was wearing. Headmistress Kinnera introduced him as Professor Burke, the Zoologist. There was an Indian woman standing next to him who beamed at the students and was the Botany and Plant Care teacher. She had curly black hair and was wearing a top hat like a nineties warlock. It looked like nobody had given her the memo that it was a new millenium.

Headmistress Kinnera was the last to step forward. Ember almost rolled her eyes at the cheesiness. She had the feeling that Headmistress Kinnera didn't like her much, but she still didn't understand why.

"Boys and girls, I welcome you to your Initiation as you embark on a new journey. I know that many of you believe that your destiny was cut short the moment you failed to be inducted as Witchies." She paused, and an uncomfortable silence descended in the crowd as the students were forced to reckon with their failure. Kinnera smiled as if nothing were amiss. "But let me tell you, the opportunities in front of you are as vast as the ocean. A worker ant is often disregarded in favor of others whose jobs are deemed more important, but the colony will fall apart the moment they stop working."

She took a dramatic pause before continuing. "Remnants are no different. People might see your powers as troubling, destructive even, but you're the glue that holds the magic and human communities together. I can say the same for our few non-magic students. When you graduate, you'll become capable members of the *human* society, no longer a threat to it. We are here to make the process of assimilation easier." She stressed the word "human" and Ember knew it was intentional.

Ember's stomach roiled. She had no intention of going back to the human world, not when there was a vast, endless world of magic rippling at her feet. She just needed a way in.

Kinnera continued. "All we ask in return is discipline as we mold you to become the best version of yourself. And now for rules—" She clapped her hands twice, and almost immediately a rolled parchment landed in Ember's lap.

"Number one, and most important, you shall wear the talisman around your neck at all times, except if asked by an instructor. Failure to do so might get you suspended or worse."

Chloe raised her hand. "Even those of us without power?"

A few snickers followed her question.

"Yes," Headmistress Kinnera said. "Which brings us to number two: you must never display your powers, unless in the presence of your instructor in a controlled environment." She looked right at Nadie when she said it, who seemed to feign innocence. What was that about?

"I mean, you already told us we can't take our talismans off. Aren't the two rules the same then?" Parker drawled.

Kinnera's jaw ticked. "Yes.

"Number three, you must never step into the Whispering Woods." Another pause. "Lest it devours you."

Kinnera got the reaction she wanted when a wave of gasps echoed around the amphitheater.

The headmistress was smirking. "The wood is a living, breathing thing, and it was designed to keep the remnants inside its boundaries. Your powers are no match for it, and in fact will just further antagonize the forest. It is true that it was created by a sorcerer, but it has found its own will since. Ancient magic thrives in its depths, far beyond our scope and that of the world we know. Even full-fledged sorcerers have no control over it, for the most part. If you fear for your life, you'll stay out of it."

Ember thought it must be her imagination, but the headmistress looked straight at her when she spoke.

"Come now, children," she said, not taking her eyes off Ember. "Let's gather around for your Initiation pictures. Line up in three files, tallest to the back and shortest to the front."

"I think it's very unfair that the forest has a grudge against us," Chloe said. "As if we didn't have enough problems." She paused as if remembering that she wasn't talking to Ember anymore.

"Listen, Chloe—" she began. The shorter girl looked up from where she was unraveling her ponytail. The two girls were getting ready to retire after a hearty dinner that consisted of a thick chicken stew and soft cooked rice with a platter of vegetables. Ember shook her head, thinking better of it. It was a good thing that Chloe wasn't making any attempts to talk to her or be her friend as she'd earlier intended.

Kinnera had said nothing about the terms of a potential transfer. She had only spoken about punishment for bad behavior as if that were all she expected from the juvenile remnants. Even non-magics were treated as more of an afterthought. Kinnera hadn't addressed any of them separately. Ember couldn't help but wonder how many more of them there were apart from Chloe.

"How do you think the trees sense when a remnant walks into the forest?" Chloe said.

"I'm sure there's a joke somewhere in there," Ember said, shimmying into her pajamas and tucking into her bed. Faithfully, Toasty hopped onto her belly. "Joke. Joke. Joke," he croaked.

"I don't get it," Chloe said, sounding confused. Ember was relieved that Chloe was at least talking to her again, even though she didn't quite meet her eyes when she did.

They had fallen into a comfortable pattern of mundane conversations. Ember was okay with that. She didn't want to ice Chloe out for the rest of her time at Glofiara. But she needed to figure a way out of there. Were there bridge exams she could take? Perhaps she could take the test of age again in a few months? Could Kinnera put in a good word for her? Ember shuddered at the possibility.

"Goodnight, Chloe," Ember said. She was so tired that she didn't remember falling asleep.

Chapter Five

Facing Magical History

The next morning, Ember woke up late. The sun was shining brightly outside the window when she sat up in her bed with a gasp. Chloe was standing just inches away from her face. Chloe stepped back. "Oh good, you're awake. We have our first class in ten minutes."

Toasty leaped onto the bedstead and croaked. "Class. Class. Class." He was almost as bad as a blaring alarm.

"That's enough, Toasty." Ember groaned under her breath as she started rummaging for clothes in her suitcase. She had already made a scene yesterday, and she didn't want to cause any more trouble if she really wanted to go to Zanith.

The floating signs had disappeared by the morning. They skipped breakfast and made a mad dash to the other side of the campus, crossing wraparound galleries and confusing, identical corridors. Ember swore the school wasn't as big yesterday, the staircases and hallways almost never-ending.

"Wait," Chloe said. "We can just ask the bricks to help us."

She stepped on one three times and said, "Take me to Facing History."

Almost immediately, the brick came to life, dragging her down the hallway. Ember didn't waste any time and followed suit. The moment the brick came to life, she thought she would almost lose her footing. But she somehow managed to find her balance, and after that it was surprisingly fun.

A short, balding man with a tailcoat was already at the board, his nasally voice droning as he recited historical facts. Chloe and Ember walked in only to realize that they recognized no one from the Initiation yesterday.

"This isn't our class," Chloe muttered under her breath.

"I can see that," Ember said. The two girls took a few steps back, smiling awkwardly at the older students who were staring at them. They took off again, and thankfully found their class just in time.

Ember took a seat in the middle row, observing her classmates. Parker and his friends were sitting at the very back, snickering amongst themselves. Elias, as expected, was sitting at the front, his notebook and textbooks out.

Ember stared down at her own copy of Facing History. It had been delivered to her the night before. Ember didn't like being reminded how easy it was for people when they could simply summon their powers and use them for good rather than, say, accidentally burning your hair off.

The teacher, a broad-spectacled man that Ember had noticed during Initiation, came into class. He unfurled a projector that was set up in front and sat down on the chair. "I'm Professor Eisenhoff, and I shall be teaching today's lecture."

The students acknowledged him as he prepared for the class.

"Remnants have caused chaos in the human world through the ages, almost exposing our world to humankind," he began.

The projector started to play with a groaning sound. The first slide was of a flood-bloated town. "East Berlin, 1868," the teacher said. "Large-scale flash floods that killed many and left several thousand people homeless. It wasn't a natural event but a Water user who lost their temper. This is what a remnant's callousness leads to—death and destruction."

The slides continued to play. One was a massive, collapsed bridge with cars piled up on either side; the next was the Leaning Tower of Pisa.

"That's right," the teacher said. "The inclination isn't natural, as claimed by many experts. Originally the remnants were employed at the Conservation Society as well, until it became apparent that they caused more problems than they solved. And the worst part is that nobody could tame these juveniles." With that, he shot a look at the class.

Parker's hand shot up midway through the lecture.

"Yes?" the instructor asked in an irritated voice.

"Is there anybody who actually wants us here?" he asked. "So far what we have learned is just how much destruction a remnant can bring."

"It's important for us to study history if you have any hopes of rejoining society when older," the teacher remarked.

"That doesn't answer my question at all," Parker said. Ember glanced back at him once. He smirked right at her, which made Ember's cheeks burn.

The next class was Natural Care of Plants and Animals. According to the naturalist who guided them into a large greenhouse, the syllabus for the semester was divided into two parts, with plant care taking two days a week and animal care the other two.

"Herbs are an important factor in healing magic," Professor Patel recited. She was the same Indian woman Ember had spotted during the Initiation. "Nature has given us all we need to take care of ourselves. But as it can give, so can it take. So it becomes important for us to distinguish between the good and the bad, lest we accidentally end up ingesting poison thinking that it is tasty chocolate berries."

"Are the trees here the same ones planted in the forest?" Elias asked, nodding at their surroundings.

The teacher shook her head. "The species and fauna that populate the forest are unlike anything found elsewhere. The few scientists that have done extensive research have found them to be a mutated genus."

"Why does that happen?" Ember couldn't resist asking.

"Each ecosystem has a particular chain through which its flora evolves. We have little control over the forest, and little knowledge of the chain that drives it. Like Headmistress Kinnera said, it has a mind of its own. All plants that we see around us are alive, but the forest is a sentient being with heart—some would say far cleverer than even a white sorcerer. It's not easily outwitted."

Ember frowned. "Does that mean even sorcerers aren't able to enter it? I thought it was only remnants that couldn't."

Professor Patel nodded. "You're right, the forest was designed to keep remnants out, but it doesn't take kindly to any sort of outside interference. While theoretically, a sorcerer with years of training and experience would be able to go in and out, it might not be so practical for them either. The forest paths are treacherous. We do not have an accurate map of—" She was momentarily distracted by a tattooed man who came in with a bag of manure. "Yes, thank you, Travis." Ember remembered the lanky man—Professor Burke—from the Initiation.

"You're welcome, Priya," the Zoo-Keep said with a grin before walking away.

"And what lies inside the forest?" Chloe asked.

The teacher looked at her for a few moments. "No one truly knows. It's vast and unending, and magic has a way of making a home in it. Now, I don't want any of you kids getting any ideas about going out there. It means nothing good."

"I heard this one kid decided to go into the forest on a bet, and when he came back, he was never right in the head again," said a high-pitched, nasally voice from behind. It was Clarisse. Ember rolled her eyes at her over-the-top story. This girl could go nowhere without calling attention to herself. "Said that he ran into someone called the Bookkeeper or whatever and they dumped a load of bugs on him," she was saying.

Ember was disgusted that Clarisse had a couple of kids enthralled. "What happened then?" asked one of the kids.

"Some say he went insane; some say that the ghosts of the forest still follow him around," Clarisse said in a mock whisper. "He kept saying that he had been imprisoned by an Ancient One deep in the heart of the forest before he managed to escape."

Ember snorted. What a load of toad dung.

She moved ahead, observing the rows of the small plants interspersed with larger trees. Up ahead, Parker was poking one of the gnarly-looking plants with a pencil.

Elias walked up to Parker and said, "Hey, you aren't supposed to do that."

"Relax, nerd. It's fine."

"You can put yourself and the others around you in danger."

"It's just a plant," Parker said, rolling his eyes.

"I'm not a botany expert, but the plant resembles Carnitharus Eucalypti, a plant known for its deadly fumes," Elias said, quite haughtily.

"You just said you're not an expert, so you can't possibly know," Parker shot back. As if to antagonize Elias, he poked a plant with his elbow.

"You shouldn't mess with things according to your whimsy," Elias said. The two boys glared at each other.

"Do I have to get your permission now?" Parker said.

Elias folded his arms in front of his chest. "As a matter of fact, you do. Professor Patel just put me in charge of the class."

Parker kept his gaze on Elias while he poked the plant again. Elias glared at him. "Stop that."

"What are you going to do about it?" Parker countered, pulling himself to his tallest height. The tension between them was thicker than a fondant cake. It felt like the start of an imminent fight. The other kids seemed to notice that as well, because they started gathering around them in a circle.

"You arrogant, pompous—" Elias said, moving around them.

Just then, Professor Patel broke into the circle and stood between the two of them. "That's enough, boys. I won't have you fighting in my class. I know plants that will make sure you have a splitting headache for days to come. Do you want that?"

"No," Parker and Elias said in unison. They took a few steps back from each other, but Ember could tell that the animosity between them was far from over.

Their Cartography teacher went on and on about how they needed to make a decision on the major they would be choosing, although that wasn't until next semester. The purpose of this, as he explained, was so that the students could close in on the role they were supposed to be majoring in for their assimilation into human society. All over the world, remnants were posted in important positions so that they could guide human society towards a better future or keep an eye on monsters lurking in the dark.

See a politician who's adamant on bringing a Green Policy change? They're probably a remnant put there by the diviners who see great catastrophe in the future if climate change isn't dealt with properly. A remnant can be a sports person reporting to the Warlocks about a Wendigo that might be trying to hurt people. They can even be a lowly clerk who helps people with their debts while keeping an eye on goblins or monsters that might be taking advantage of them. Regardless of what role you choose; the final step is integration into human society.

Ember was not interested in any of that. She wanted to be on the other side, fighting the monsters, not just reporting them. She wanted to be a sorcerer. And what had she done about that so far? Absolutely nothing.

"It's all just to keep us in line," Parker was saying on the way out. "It's all propaganda."

"It's not like we can do anything about it," Clarisse said. "It's just the way it has been. Even Chancellor Yuleik agrees."

Ember recognized the name even though she had never met the man before. He was the current head of the Ether Conservation Society who had won the position after gaining the vote of confidence last fall. She had seen his posters all over the place promising changes, unlike his predecessor, who had been the head for the last decade. Nothing much had changed since then.

"Chancellor Yuleik is a different man," one of Clarisse's cronies was saying.

"My parents say that he's as arrogant as they come," Clarisse said. "I wouldn't pin too much hope on him, but maybe he'll be harder on the ones who are the worst." She looked at Ember when she said that, a smirk playing on her lips.

Ember rolled her eyes. *We are all the worst; that's why we are here*, she thought.

By the time Ember walked into the last class of the day, she was tired and hungry. The class was held on the fourth-floor east wing, a dome-shaped room painted in gold that looked identical to the amphitheater downstairs, minus the grandeur.

There were no chairs or desks in the class, and Ember mused to herself that since the class was called Creativity, they would have to fashion chairs, kind of like carpentry. A few students were absent, including Chloe, and Ember realized that this was the only class that was exclusively meant for the remnants.

Maybe we'll actually learn something useful here, Ember thought to herself. This was the class she had been waiting for. A strange buzz took over her arms as she walked in, wondering who would be teaching the class.

Minutes passed, and when it began to be apparent that nobody was coming, the children grew rowdier by the second. Ember sat in a corner of the room, her knees pulled up to her chest. All she could think about was food.

"Come on," Parker said, taking his talisman off. "There's no teacher here, and we should introduce ourselves by showcasing our powers. Besides, this class is called Creativity for a reason."

Elias walked past him with books folded under his chest. "A few monkeys will get the rest of us in trouble."

"I think we'll be fine if some people keep their mouths shut," Parker added, looking straight at Elias, who glared at him. The cold war brewing between them couldn't be more evident.

Most of the kids agreed with Parker. Some of them had picked up a model of the globe and were taking turns playing with it like it was a game of ball. A Wind user was floating it above their head but ended up splatting it on their face, while an Ice user was trying to freeze it and accidentally ended up shooting ice at the ceiling.

Parker stood in the middle of the small circle of his friends, coming in and out of focus. He had the power of Invisibility, but it didn't seem to help him much.

"Why are you here cowering in the corner, Pearson?" Clarisse said, walking up to her. "Not interested in playing?"

Ember said a curse word in Hungarian that she had picked up from a mission. Clarisse frowned at her. "I know you think you're all that, but trust me—"

"I have nothing to prove to you," Ember said flatly.

Clarisse smirked at her. "I know all about you. You're the worst one out of all of us. The teachers were practically warning us against you."

"We're all remnants here, if you haven't noticed," Ember pointed out.

Clarisse took a menacing step towards her. "I've heard about what you did at the Conservation Society. There are rumors that you almost burned down the Ceremony Hall, and they had to close it for two weeks to restore it."

Ember narrowed her eyes. "You don't know that."

"You better not cross me again, or I won't keep my mouth shut, Fire freak. I know what you did during your test of age," Clarisse said with a menacing smile. "Even your little minion would be scared of you if she knew."

Ember stayed silent, her mind racing. How did Clarisse discover her secret? Ember's parents had sworn that it wouldn't come out. If the teachers at Glofiara found out, she could kiss any future at Zanith goodbye.

Ember watched as Elias narrowly missed a levitating compass while he walked from one side of the room to the other, seemingly unscathed by the war waging around him. He did it twice with two different objects. Ember frowned. Elias had dodged the objects without even sparing a glance at them. Which meant that her prediction was right, and he indeed was a psychic or a clairvoyant of some sort.

Someone cleared their throat loudly. Ember turned toward the sound. Nadie stood at the door, her arms crossed in front of her chest. Most of the children hadn't noticed her there. The room was a chaos of unreliable powers zapping, a half-frozen ceiling, wind-scattered papers in the room, and a kid levitating in midair inside an unstable astral projection, amongst other things.

"Professor Owsmann," Ember called loudly, which seemed to finally catch the attention of everyone in the class. Today Nadie was wearing a patchwork jacket with matching trousers, and her hair was coiled behind her in a perfect swooping bun. The water bubble burst suddenly, splashing on everyone in the room. Some of it landed on Nadie, but she remained unfazed. The wind died down, and the levitating kid fell to the ground with a loud crash, but he appeared unhurt mostly. It looked like a tornado had gone through the room, leaving disaster in its wake. Suddenly, Ember realized why the Society would want to keep the remnants inside a forest full of vicious trees.

"Clean up your mess," Professor Owsmann said simply. She had no anger in her voice. She didn't scream or shout; her command was simple. The students glanced at each other. "You've been told about the consequences of your actions, but you never listened. Now it's time to do just that. Start cleaning up after yourselves."

The bubble of inactivity broke, and all of them jumped into action. Professor Owsmann watched them silently. It took everybody a good hour to clean up everything and return the room to its initial state. Ember helped with the floor-cleaning, and Elias rearranged a sheaf of papers.

"This is what you did to the room in the ten minutes I was gone," Nadie said. "Imagine what you will do if you're sent out into the world with uncontrolled powers. I know many of you resent this place—" She looked straight at Ember when she spoke. "But understand that everybody here at Glofiara is working for your own good."

"We didn't mean to," one of the kids said.

"I don't want your apologies," Professor Owsmann said. "But you must all be aware of what your magic can do if left unchecked. I want you to reflect on that when you go back to your respective dorms tonight."

As if on cue, the distant groan of the bell rang, announcing the end of the period. The students started shuffling out. "She's weird but in a cool way," someone said. Ember couldn't agree more. Even though Nadie's methods were unconventional, she got her point across better than any other teacher on the campus, whose only motives seemed to be to terrify the remnants.

"Ember, a minute, please," Professor Owsmann called out.

Ember groaned to herself. She thought Nadie had forgotten about her punishment by now.

Elias gave her an apologetic look. "Best of luck."

Chapter Six

A White Lie

"I didn't do anything today, Professor Owsmann," Ember said, walking up to her.

"I know," she said. "And you can just call me Nadie." She had a willowy frame, and she was a whole foot taller than Ember.

Ember stared at her teacher suspiciously. There was no way she could be so nice when the other teachers were practically hostile. "So what's it going to be?" Ember asked as Nadie's words about facing up to consequences swam in her head. She had a few ideas in mind—she had heard about the fishy hallway, a corridor that always smelled of fish on the fifth floor, or maybe it would be to clean up Headmistress Kinnera's office, or something equally bad.

"So what do you prefer—tea or coffee? I'm partial to lavender tea. It helps soothe my nerves," Nadie said, gesturing at Ember to follow her to a door that opened up to a smaller room.

Ember gaped at her as she walked behind Nadie into a dimly lit space. The windows were shut, and a big oak desk took over most of the space. It had a clutter of various assortments and parchments topped with quill and paper. There was a cozy fireplace on the other side, the hearth of which was currently empty. "Professor Owsmann?" Ember said, feeling out of sorts.

"Just Nadie, please, and it gets really drafty up here," Nadie explained. She walked up to the small stove next to her desk and put a pot of water to boil. The sweet smell of lavender wafted over to Ember, who felt immediately at ease.

"Aren't you going to punish me?" Ember couldn't help but ask.

Nadie raised a brow. "Do you want me to?"

"I assume that's why you instructed me to stay back after class."

Nadie's brows kept rising till they almost disappeared into her hairline. Finally, she said, "No, I didn't call you here to punish you. But we still need to talk about what happened yesterday. I promised Mother Irene."

Ember shuffled her feet. "I know I shouldn't have done that. I was just trying to protect my roommate."

"I understand that, but you cannot let your emotions make your decisions. It takes years of practice for a full-fledged ether user to perfect their craft, and it's especially difficult for a remnant when the odds are stacked against you," Nadie said, her voice not unkind. "I know that it seems the world is out to get you, but it's the opposite of what I want, especially in my class. I know how hard it is to be treated as different." It sounded like Nadie spoke from experience, but Ember knew that all the teachers at the school were warlocks, maybe some had even leveled up to being diviners. Nadie would never understand.

"So why am I here?" Ember asked.

"For tea, of course," Nadie said, lighting up. Just then, the kettle came to a boil.

"Can I ask you something?"

"Sure, go on," Nadie said, pouring the tea into two cute little cups.

"We're not supposed to take off our talismans at any point, right? So after what happened in class today, aren't we supposed to be punished?"

"You forgot the exception," Nadie said.

Ember frowned. "But you weren't present in the class."

"Wasn't I?" Nadie said with a wink.

Ember's eyes widened. "Oh my Ethilenne, you planned it?"

Nadie nodded. "It's not healthy to keep your powers hidden. Magic, especially erratic magic, can't be suppressed forever. Sooner or later, it will spill out in an even more destructive way. The rules at Glofiara—and the Society itself—are rather stringent, and if it were up to me, things would be quite different. But don't let Headmistress Kinnera hear that."

"Trust me," Ember said with an un-ladylike snort. "I won't. She doesn't like me that much."

Nadie frowned. "Why do you say that?"

"No reason," Ember said hastily.

"So what was your takeaway from what happened in the class?" Nadie asked, walking to her desk.

Ember paused. "They let go of themselves."

It hadn't dawned on her until she said it, but she realized what it was—camaraderie. Despite what background people had come from, they were stuck in the same situation. They were all misfits.

Ember would never forget how her parents looked at her after the failed test of age, like she was a firecracker about to go off. She was the imperfect daughter. In some ways, that attention was worse than when they didn't pay any heed to her at all.

Ember thought back to the day when she had left the hall crying. The fire had been put out, but seven of the high Council members had escorted her to the entrance as if she were a criminal.

"I'm sorry about everything that happened," Ember's dad was saying. "She didn't mean to."

"None of them do. This is the reason they're sent to Glofiara. I recommend you do the same," one of the Council members said.

George winced, glancing at Ember once. The disappointment and wariness was clear on his face. "Are you sure?"

"She almost burned down an entire hall. Of course I'm certain," the Council member said before walking away.

"I'm sorry, Mom," Ember had said. Her mother nodded stiffly, doing nothing to console her.

Ember shook her head, coming back to the present. "All my life, my parents have taught me to be in control. My sister has the power of phase shifting, and she was just always good at it, like my parents. On the other hand, I was always a mess. It didn't help that I was a Fire user, so I could put people around me in danger with my ability," she said, the words flowing out of her. Maybe it was the lavender tea, maybe it was the way Nadie listened to her.

Nadie nodded. "I believe that the test of age alone shouldn't determine the failure or success of a person at the age of thirteen or square them off in neat little labels. It's never that easy, especially not in a thing as extraordinary as ether."

"The Conservation Society seems to think that," Ember said morosely when suddenly a thought came to her mind. "Do you think I could perhaps take the test again?"

Nadie frowned at her. "What do you mean?"

Ember swallowed hesitatingly. "I want to go to Zanith. It is my dream, but I can't, because—" She broke off, unable to get the rest of the words out. It was the first time she had said those words aloud ever since Summer had planted the idea in her head.

"I'm sorry, Ember, I don't know anything about that," Nadie said. After a pause, she added, "But maybe there is something we can do about it."

Ember's face lit up. "Really?"

Nadie shrugged. "It's definitely worth a try."

Ember was smiling by the time she left Nadie's office. She couldn't wait to return tomorrow.

When Ember came back to her room, Chloe was sitting on her bed with Toasty on her lap. "Chloe, Chloe, Chloe," Toasty croaked.

Chloe looked up and beamed at her. "I finally managed to teach him my name. Isn't that awesome?"

"Sure." Ember felt a pang of envy, which was odd, but she knew that Toasty didn't take too kindly to strangers. When they had guests wherever they were staying at that time, he was often found to have peed on the clean, white sheets. That was why Toasty and Ember got along so well, as her parents often liked to tease her.

Toasty leaped up to Ember's arm before hopping on her shoulder and nuzzling against her.

"Toasty is such a good boy. You don't mind that I fed him a bit of raisin, do you?"

"Not at all," Ember said. She didn't want to tell Chloe that raisins were one of Toasty's favorite foods. No wonder he was already smitten with Chloe.

"You missed high tea," Chloe said hesitantly. "Where were you?"

"Nadie—well, Professor Owsmann had me stay back," Ember said with a shrug.

Chloe flinched, and her face crumpled. "It's all because of me."

Ember realized that Chloe probably thought that Nadie had punished her. She nodded. "I had a horrible time indeed. She made me sit on my knees and practice cosmo-arithmetic on the floor and berated me when I didn't know the complex forms of candela."

Chloe's eyes watered. "I'm sorry."

Ember rushed to her, shaking her head. "I was only kidding, Chloe. Nadie was very nice to me. She even made me tea." Chloe was too sensitive for her own good.

"You don't have to lie to me, you know? I'm a big girl. I'll be turning twelve next month."

"Twelve?" Ember said, frowning. "How were you able to take the test of age then? You can't take it before thirteen unless you are exceptionally—"

"Gifted," Chloe said. "I know that." Usually, an ether user's abilities got better over time until turning thirteen, when you came of age in the community. But some children showed prowess over their ability since they were as little as two months old. They were deemed Gifted. Summer was one of them. She had taken the test at ten and passed with flying colors.

Chloe fell silent, and Ember could understand that she didn't want to elaborate. She had so many questions about Chloe, but what was the point when she would be leaving soon?

Nadie seemed sincere enough, and once they devised a plan to get Ember into Zanith, she would be out of here.

That evening, her parents called her on the Magical Mefaroso Network. It was a device set up next to each student's bed so that their family and loved ones could reach them without human interference or entanglement. Ember had a human cellphone, as well, but her parents and relatives rarely used that.

Ember's comm-device buzzed loudly with the incoming notification. She saw the way Chloe perked up from the textbook she was reading. Ember was lying on the bed, going through the conversation she had had with Nadie earlier that day.

Chloe cleared her throat. "That's for you."

"Right," Ember said, sitting up.

She picked up the comm-device, which was shaped like P, tapering at the bottom instead of a regular human cellphone.

"Ember," said the excited voice of Rosetta Pearson right at her ear. Ember cringed before realizing that the comm-device did exactly what it advertised—*Your Loved Ones Right at Your Ears.* That was literally what it felt like.

"Hey, Mom," Ember said, sitting down on her canopy bed.

"Oh my, George, hear how clear her voice is, it's like she's standing with us," Ember's mother said to her father. "The humans should really learn to broaden their communication bandwidth."

"Actually," Ember said. "That's one way we are different from them. Our ears can pick up sounds at greater hertz than they can. In fact, our hearing range is closer to the canine species than a human."

"Look how much she's learning at school already!" Rosetta said. "I knew Glofiara would be good for you."

Ember wasn't so sure about that.

"So are you on your way to Peru?" she asked. They were about to embark on a new mission that would take them all the way down to the South Pole.

"Actually," George said. "There's been a slight change of plans."

"They're with me!" came Summer's sing-songy voice that made Ember groan.

"Excuse me?" she asked.

"Mom and Dad were supposed to leave yesterday, but they decided to stay back and spend the day with me in New York. I'm posted here for my training."

"Wow," Ember said sarcastically, her words as rough as sandpaper. "That sounds great." That didn't, in fact, sound great to her.

Growing up, Ember had felt like an outsider in her own family. It wasn't that her parents didn't love her—there wasn't much time to do it when they had a Gifted daughter whose abilities demanded their attention. When Ember was three, Summer, who was only four years older than her, had started showing remarkable abilities. It had started with her walking into walls. Even Summer had no idea what she could do until one day when Ember and her family had been invited to a neighbor's home. They were hunting a wish-granting leprechaun, but they couldn't keep turning down invitations. They had to blend in, and that meant playing nice with the neighbors.

While the neighbor—Ember couldn't remember their name—got out drinks, Summer had followed them, but instead of the door, she had walked in through the wall. Their neighbors were, of course, flabbergasted and practically petrified by this. Ember's parents called on Society members to deal with the mess and, in their hurry to get away, left Ember behind.

She wasn't discovered until a few hours later. By then, the neighbors' memories had been zapped and they had no idea she was at their home or how she had ended up there. Her parents hadn't even noticed that Ember was missing for those four hours. Their focus had been on Summer. She was just like them, her powers manifesting effortlessly while Ember's were a total dud.

It had always been her parents and Summer against her. Growing up, they would always compare the two—look, she learned to walk through solid walls when she was six and she didn't even mean to, look how perfect her hair is when she's tossing it over her shoulder like she's in a movie. They didn't actually say the latter, but that was what Ember thought.

Summer always had things easy; she woke up looking perfect every morning, while Ember was greeted with a new zit ever since she had turned thirteen.

"New York is so beautiful," Summer said. "I wish you were here."

"Sure," Ember said. She was already bored of the conversation. Any moment now, Summer would go off about how perfect her first day training as an apprentice at the Conservation Society had been.

But instead, she surprised her by saying, "So, how are things at Glofiara?"

"It's exactly as bad as it sounds," Ember said. "But there is a silver lining. Summer, I think I've found a way to get into Zanith."

There was a short pause before Summer said, "What do you mean?"

"I was saying that maybe there's a way I could get into Zanith, you know? I spoke to one of my teachers and she seems to agree."

"I'm sure she was just trying to be kind," Summer said.

"You mean to say she was patronizing to me?" Ember said, her temper flaring. "Well, dear sister, you will be glad to know that you're wrong this time."

"Ember, what you're saying is impossible," Summer said. Ember could almost picture her sister shaking her head.

Ember gritted her teeth. "You're the one who told me I could. Are you seriously going back on your word now? Or do you think I simply can't do it?" She had that familiar urge to scream. Her body grew painfully hot, and her skin reddened.

Toasty hopped up on her thighs and fixed her with a concerned stare that seemed to help with her growing anger. The last thing she needed was to accidentally light her bed on fire. Even Chloe was watching her. "Are you okay?" she mouthed.

Ember didn't answer and turned to her sister. "Well?"

Summer sighed insufferably. Her voice dropped before she spoke again. "Listen, it was just something I made up so that I could convince you to go to Glofiara."

Ember blanched. "You did what?"

"It was just supposed to be a simple white lie," Summer said. "I didn't actually mean it. Ember, you have to understand that in the history of Zanith, no remnant has ever set foot in its halls."

"You're lying."

"I'm not. The Society doesn't let you take your test of age twice," Summer said. "I'm sorry if I made you feel otherwise. I just don't want you to get your hopes up. There's a reason that remnants are housed at Glofiara. You'll be safer there, from yourself."

Ember's ears buzzed. Summer spoke like everybody else. Ember thought that at least she had her sister on her side, but she was mistaken. She saw her as the troublemaker everybody else did. She had lied, and it was another trick to make her fall in line. Ember wanted to scream.

I don't deserve any of this. I haven't done anything wrong. I don't want to be shunned because of the stupid rules of the Society. I'm not dangerous; I'm just a kid. Help me.

Instead, she said, "I have to go."

"Ember, wait—" Summer started, but Ember deactivated her comm-device and put it away.

"Is everything okay?" Chloe asked, peering at her curiously.

Ember was almost on the verge of tears, and she never cried easily. Summer had lied to her so that it would be easier to send her away. And now that she was gone for good, her family was having a blast. It was like she'd never really existed, like she was never a part of the family.

Her comm-device pinged with a new status update from the Magic-Net community. Despite herself, she clicked on the link and regretted it almost instantaneously.

It was a picture of her parents and Summer hugging each other amidst the full bloom of Central Park. The comments below it read:

Such a perfect, beautiful family!
You must be so proud of your daughter.
She has taken right after you. Big shoes to fill, Summer!!!

It was the same as always: the other daughter didn't exist.

Chapter Seven

OPEN HEART

Ember spent the next day in a foul mood, barely paying attention to her classes. She would occasionally tune in and hear bits and pieces, like when Professor Detteo, their Physi-Magical Sciences teacher, taught them about the remnant phenomenon. He was wearing the same argyle sweater from Initiation, and considering the state of his mop of curls, Ember couldn't help but wonder if he had since taken a shower.

"Nobody really knows why remnants exist," he said. "It's a bizarre phenomenon unexplained by science. Over centuries, many brilliant scholars have performed experiments to understand how magic passes down through families. In 1967, there was a promising paper that claimed that there were certain gene markers that put remnants apart from the rest of the magic-users just as it made us different from humans, but it was later debunked, particularly with regards to the existence of non-magic people in our community."

In the front row, Elias was bent over his desk, taking notes. Ember was surprised that his quill didn't break. He wrote with breakneck speed as if his life depended on it.

Ember was past caring about her existence. What did it matter why she didn't have powers that could actually work in her favor? The fact was that she didn't. She had heard the story several times.

She was distracted even in Creativity Class, where Nadie divided them into groups of four, according to their abilities—elemental, physical, natural and spiritual. Obviously, it was just four broad categories, but magic found a way to overlap, and sometimes some people were known to master more than one power.

Elemental magic, like Ember's, was the most common. Then came abilities like shape-shifting that came under the physical category, animal influence under the natural category, and the rarest form of magic was spiritual, which included powers like emotional manipulation, astral projection, or conduits like Nadie who could either be a conductor or an inductor.

Ember was surprised to see Chloe and the rest of the non-magics in the class when they had been glaringly absent the previous day. Poor Chloe stood to the side, not knowing where to go.

"I-I don't think I really fit in anywhere," she said miserably. A few of the kids snickered, including Clarisse. Parker elbowed her in the side.

"She's here to fill up the non-magic quota," Clarisse said loudly enough for the entire class to hear. Chloe looked like she wanted to melt into the floor. Ember glared at the pair.

"Clarisse, you're a remnant. You of all people should understand what it's like to be different," Nadie said. "It isn't kind to treat others as beneath you," she continued. "That's not what magic teaches us. Besides, I called them here. I want all the students, remnant or otherwise, to be present for the demonstration, and I know each of you will have something useful to add to the class."

"It's pointless to have non-magics in a class meant for power demonstration, isn't it?" Clarisse shot back.

"Do you mean to question your teacher?" Nadie said. Clarisse's mouth closed.

Ember smirked.

"You can pick any group you want," Nadie said kindly to Chloe.

"Really?" Chloe asked, her eyes widening.

Ember beamed at Nadie. She was so unlike the rest of the teachers at Glofiara.

Chloe hesitantly walked over to the Spiritual remnants and stood at the back of the line. There were only five of them, but they welcomed her gratefully. They were easily outnumbered by the Elementals five to one.

"And now what?" Clarisse said. "Are we supposed to fight each other for total dominion?"

"We all know who's going to win," a boy Ember didn't know by name called out from the Elemental line.

"Do I really have to participate in this violent exercise?" Elias asked.

"There's not going to be any violent display of power. I want you to face the person next to you, shake hands, and sit on the floor," Nadie said.

"That sounds stupid," one of Clarisse's cronies said.

The children reluctantly sat on the floor. Nadie watched them with a satisfied smile on her face. "And now," she said, "I want you to close your eyes and focus."

Well, that was anticlimactic. Ember was waiting for something cool to happen, but Nadie just wanted them to meditate. Ember thought about her sister, and how she had already joined her apprenticeship, while Ember was being taught ways to tamp down her power.

"Ember," Nadie called. "You're stressed. Try to relax and see with your mind's eye instead. Open your heart, and let your powers take over. It's overwhelming at first, but I promise you'll be fine."

Ember grumbled but followed Nadie's instruction anyway. She closed her eyes and concentrated. Nothing new happened on the first day, which was expected. A Wind user accidentally banged one of the windows off its hinges while another almost created a mud storm until Nadie stopped it. By the time the class was over, the room was in a state of disarray as if it had passed through the eye of a storm. Nadie didn't seem to be deterred, however.

"This," Ember thought to herself. "This is why we are at Glofiara."

The next few days passed in a blur. During classes, Ember did her best to concentrate, and afterwards, she would stay up in Nadie's office, talking to her for hours. In the week that passed, Ember noticed a shift within herself. The anger she had felt for her parents when they dropped her off at Glofiara was dimming, which made it easier to concentrate on Nadie's lessons during the Creativity class. That was her favorite part of the day.

At first, Ember didn't feel any differently during the meditation sessions. But then as her body relaxed, a different kind of energy began to take over. A peaceful energy. She was humming from inside. But otherwise, nothing else happened that day. Nothing changed on the second day either. By the end of the second week, she was used to the new energy. In fact, she welcomed it, opening her heart to it instead of simply being afraid. Finally, Ember opened her eyes and, as if she knew just what to do, she looked down at her finger, where a tiny ember pulsed and danced.

Ember stared at it with fascination and awe. She had never been able to produce something so tiny and contained. Her powers usually went from zero to one hundred until they eventually got out of control.

"Good job, Ember," Nadie said. Ember beamed. For as long as she could remember, she had feared what she could do instead of being excited about it. Nadie had managed to banish that fear to a corner of her heart until the positive overwhelmed it. "I knew you could do it."

Ember smiled. Maybe this was what she had been missing—a little encouragement. Around her, the other children seemed to have the same experience. Well, most of them. Elias sat stonily on the floor while the boy next to him floated in midair. Unlike the first few days, his astral projection wasn't unstable.

"The point of the exercise is to demonstrate that the calmer your mind is, the better control you have of your body," Nadie said, looking pleased with their progress. "It knows what to do. Your ancestors have passed down their powers, preserving them through you. Humans call it intuition."

Just as quickly as the flame had appeared, it went away, leaving Ember cold in its wake.

"A steady mind lets you have controlled access to your powers for short periods of time. This is the first step, of course, and we have a long way to go."

The bell rang, and Nadie stepped back. Ember couldn't stop gaping at her. She had just opened her up to a whole new world of possibilities. This time, Nadie didn't have to ask her to stay back.

"Did you give it any thought?" Ember asked as Nadie unlocked her office door. She put an unusually ornate key away in the pocket of her skirt.

"What about?" Nadie asked. They had spent the last week in mostly silence as Nadie gave her odd jobs that needed to be done—mostly cataloging. But Ember couldn't keep her excitement in check, especially not after she had managed to summon the controlled flame. Maybe there was hope for her after all.

"Me getting into Zanith?" Ember asked hopefully. Just because Summer didn't know of a way for a remnant to get into Zanith, didn't mean it was impossible. Ember wasn't going to let Summer's words get her down.

Nadie bit her lip. "I don't know about that."

Ember's face fell. "But you promised me help."

"I did," Nadie said, nodding. "But I don't think I've come across anybody who managed to transform from a remnant to a fledgling witch after failing the test of age. Trust me, I've spent the last week looking up information on this." So Nadie hadn't forgotten.

Ember's shoulders slumped. Her hope seeped out of her.

"But we can still try!" said Nadie.

"How?"

"The library, of course," Nadie said matter-of-factly. "We can find all our answers in books."

Ember wasn't convinced. She wasn't very fond of reading anyway. Before she could say anything, there was a knock at the door, and moments later, Professor Detteo walked in. He had finally combed his hair, and he was holding a bouquet of wildflowers.

He froze when he saw Ember standing next to Nadie, and a faint blush crept up his face. He was so pale that Ember was reminded of the tomatoes she had seen in Spain.

"Professor Nadie, I didn't know you had c-company," Professor Detteo stammered.

Ember smirked. This was the most interesting thing that had happened to her in a while.

"Ember is in my care. As the first-year mother, I'm supposed to be responsible for her detention."

Professor Detteo frowned at Ember. "It has just been two weeks," he said.

"That's me, I guess," Ember said, shrugging. "Always getting into trouble."

"Nonsense," Nadie said and then turned to Detteo. "I think she's turning out to be one of my favorites."

Ember's heart leaped. She had never been a particular favorite of anybody.

Nadie, who was beaming down at her, turned to face Detteo again. "But what brings you to my office?"

Detteo cleared his throat. He thrust the flowers at her. Nadie blinked at them in shock before accepting them gratefully and sniffing deeply. They smelled more pungent than sweet, but Nadie seemed pleased. She walked to an empty vase and put them in it carefully. Professor Detteo seemed elated.

"I thought perhaps we could make a short trip to the greenhouse. Professor Patel just had a consignment for a few new species to be brought in, and one of them is Tachkmi Hachydon, also known as Love Plant. I thought we might see them together." He sounded so hopeful.

"That sounds lovely, really," Nadie said.

"So you'll come?" he said hopefully.

"Detteo, I always have a lovely and rather educational time with you, and I really appreciate the flowers, but I'm kind of busy with something." Nadie seemed to be woefully ignorant of Professor Detteo's feelings towards her. Instead of gazing into his eyes and noticing his lovelorn gaze, she was looking at Ember.

"What say you and I do some research?" she said.

"Are you sure?" Ember asked, glancing at Detteo, who looked dejected.

"Absolutely," Nadie said. She was so focused on Ember that she barely spared him a glance.

"I guess I'll see myself out," Professor Detteo said.

"I would love to see you again sometime soon," Nadie said. Professor Detteo looked so hopeful that he almost tripped on his way out. Ember felt a pang in her heart, but she quickly forgot that when Nadie set down a couple of books on the side table.

"Maybe we should begin with these. I've always had this in my office but never really made a point to read it."

"What are we looking for exactly?" Ember asked, sitting down on one of the surprisingly comfortable wicker chairs.

"Anything to do with remnant magic, history, science, or otherwise," Nadie said.

"That seems pretty broad," Ember said, unsure.

"I know, the task ahead of us is daunting, but we need to cover our bases before we come upon any actual solution, and we can narrow things from that point. We have to do this old-school style. The Society doesn't like interference of any kind with its rigid rules."

Ember nodded. She wondered if the professor was doing all of this just to cheer her up. She hoped not. Ember didn't know what she would do if Nadie couldn't help her get into Zanith.

Chapter Eight

SECRET KEEPER

The next few weeks were spent settling into a comfortable routine at the school. Ember didn't want to admit it to her family, or herself, but she had started to like this place. Her feelings were shifting, mostly due to Nadie. They spent almost every afternoon together, either going through books, baking treats, or talking about life in general. Ember had never felt so heard or seen in her life.

Growing up, her parents had almost always been away, leaving her to the care of her older sister. And after Summer started going to Zanith, they would drag her with them to the human world, enrolling her in schools where Ember found herself woefully behind all her classmates. They found her weird, and it didn't take Ember long to realize that she had never really fit in anywhere, until now.

Almost a month to the date of their arrival, Ember stayed back after class, as was her usual routine. She was already done with her required detention, but she liked spending time with Nadie. To her surprise, today, she wasn't alone.

Parker leaned against the wall, humming to himself. Ever since the incident with Chloe, Ember greatly disliked him. She disliked all bullies. "What are you doing here?"

"I'm in detention," he said. "What are *you* doing here? Still serving detention for threatening to burn us?"

He was obviously trying to get a reaction out of her. "I never threatened you," she said. "You shouldn't make picking on the weak a personality trait."

His face darkened. "I had no idea she was a non-magic."

"Would that have changed things?" Ember shot back.

Parker faced away, so Ember guessed that for him the conversation was over. Nadie returned after a few minutes, her light orange jacket swishing around her as she walked. She had such a cool aesthetic and vibe around her. People would usually find it weird, and Ember had heard people gossiping about her on multiple occasions, but there was something in the way Nadie carried herself that just worked. "Oh, good, there's two of you today. I have some admin work I need to get done."

Great, Parker showing up had already started to change things for the worse. Ember glared at his back as she followed him into the office.

Nadie nodded at the pile of old notebooks. "I'm helping Professor Patel rearrange her logbooks. She obviously can't do it alone, since there are over one million plants and species known to our kind. I've offered to help her, but since I don't have the power of speed, I need some assistance."

"Boring," Parker said, yawning under his breath.

"Would you rather mop the floors then?" Nadie said. "Or perhaps you would like to work at the manure house down at the Menagerie." The Menagerie was a small enclosure at the back of the school grounds where the school Zoologist, or Zoo-Keep, tended to a small group of animals. They were yet to start animal care study in the semester, so Ember and her classmates had actually never been down there. Ember had spotted it from her window at the tower, and from such a distance, sometimes she couldn't tell where the Menagerie ended and the vast, endless forest began.

Parker had the exact opposite reaction either were expecting. "Really?" His voice perked up.

"Do you like working with animals, Parker?"

"Yes," Parker grudgingly admitted. "I had one—" He looked up at Ember, who was staring at him, and seemed to think better of what he was about to say. She wondered what he had done to end up in detention, like her.

Ember, Parker, and Nadie worked for the next hour. She treated them to honey rosemary cake and a fizzy drink, and the combination was surprisingly good. After their time was up, Nadie let them go.

Ember hung back, waiting for Parker to leave. She collected her things slowly, and as soon as he was out, she turned to Nadie. "So why is he here?"

"I don't know the details, but Mother Irene told me that he pranked a fellow first-year," Nadie said.

Ember briefly wondered who it could have been, since Parker seemed to care little about anybody but himself. Clarisse and he, along with the rest of their cronies, were always huddled together during meals and between classes, plotting schemes. They had left her alone, thankfully, after the first incident, and Ember figured they were scared of her. They weren't the only ones. Other than Chloe, or sometimes Elias, nobody else in their year actually wanted to talk to her during the group assignments.

"Professor?" Ember asked. Something had been weighing on her for the last couple of days.

"Yes?" Nadie asked.

"Will we ever find something?" It had been almost a month since she had first come to Glofiara. Meditation had helped her stabilize her powers, but only for a few seconds. If she tried too hard, nothing happened, and it felt like things were going nowhere for her. There were no answers in the books, either, even though Nadie had promised there would be.

Nadie looked at her sympathetically. She squeezed her shoulder. "I don't want to fill you with false hope, but there is something that might help us."

"Really?"

She nodded. "I was going to wait before sharing this with you, but I had a chat with Professor Detteo the other day, and he told me that he was working with a few of his peers in the Phys-Magic community and they were trying to figure out a way to stabilize the core of a remnant's power."

Ember gaped. "Is that possible?"

"It's not clear, as of yet, but our scientific community has already made leaps and bounds in many areas, and this is just one they are delving into. It seems that the Conservation Society is a little concerned about the growing number of remnants."

"What do you mean?"

"There are many more than there used to be, and it's growing every year," Nadie said. Ember remembered a similar remark that her father had made when he was dropping her at Glofiara.

"Is ether dying?" Ember asked.

"Not at all," Nadie said hastily.

"So theoretically, if this experimental procedure is proven successful, what would it mean for us remnants?" She held in a breath, waiting for Nadie to confirm her hopes.

"It would open up many opportunities for remnants," Nadie answered.

"Maybe integration to human societies wouldn't be compulsory for remnants anymore," Ember said.

"That is very possible," Nadie said, nodding, "but integration itself isn't bad. Remnants are doing important work in the human world."

"Sure," Ember said.

"I know you don't believe that," Nadie said kindly.

Ember sighed. "It's just not the path I see for myself."

"Understood," Nadie said. She was the first person who didn't think Ember's ambitions were ridiculous, and Ember was grateful for that. "I didn't want to raise your hopes before anything happens, but Professor Detteo has closed in on markers that show great promise. In fact, he has started to study cases, and he is looking for potential candidates."

"Can I volunteer?" Ember said.

Nadie hesitated. "I don't know. You're a little young."

"Please, I just want a chance," Ember said, tears filling her eyes. She couldn't let this opportunity go; otherwise, in a few years, she would be stuck as a clerk in a boring human neighborhood. "If you don't tell him, he'll never find out."

Nadie seemed to think about it. "I guess we can try."

"Really?" Ember asked.

Nadie nodded. "Of course, but we have to keep it a secret."

The next day, when Ember went to visit Nadie, she was practically brimming with excitement. Parker was nowhere to be found, and he seemed to have skipped Creativity as well.

Nadie produced a vial with a hooked end and small pipe.

Ember looked at it curiously. "What is it?" She had noticed similar vials in the Chem-Magi lab, but never one like this.

"It can draw out a little bit of essence and hold it in," Nadie said. "Now stay still. It won't hurt."

Ember didn't even dare breathe as Nadie extracted her essence. She barely felt a pinch at her neck, and then it was over. When she looked up, Parker was standing at the door with an unreadable expression on his face. It was unclear how much he had seen or heard, but he didn't comment on it.

Nadie, meanwhile, had slipped the vial into her pocket before even Ember could see it.

"Are we continuing our work from yesterday?" Parker asked casually.

"Of course," Nadie said with a nod like nothing was amiss. Ember, on the other hand, looked like a deer caught in headlights.

"You okay, Ember?" Parker asked, smirking at her.

Instead of answering him, she marched up to her desk and started to work on the logbooks. Afterwards, when they were done, she was the first to leave. But Parker caught up to her in the hallway.

"So what black sorcerer thingy were you up to before?" Parker said.

Ember stopped walking. "What?"

"Oh, don't act coy. I saw the professor with something that she took from you. I think you sneaked illegal contraband onto campus. Nadie's too nice and obviously doesn't want to get you into trouble."

Ember continued to frown at him, until she realized that he had interpreted the situation in the wrong way. "You have no proof."

"Maybe not," he said, taking a step back. "But I have my eyes on you, Pearson. Sooner or later, I'm going to figure out your little secret."

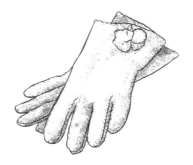

Chapter Nine

A Pixie's Vision

Parker's words followed Ember for the rest of the week. During lunch or dinner, she would often spot him smirking at her. She had no idea who he was talking to or exactly what kind of rumors he was spreading. She really didn't care what her classmates thought about her. She just didn't want to get into trouble with the headmistress.

A pixie joined Ember at the front of the queue for the food. She hadn't seen a pixie in years, not since she had been to New Zealand as a child. She hadn't known that pixies even existed in this part of the world, let alone in Glofiara. It was a shimmering being with sparkling dust scattered all over its body. It was then that Ember realized it was not a pixie at all, but Elias.

Now that she thought about it, she hadn't seen him in class yesterday. He turned to glare at her. "What are you looking at?"

"What's wrong with you?" she blurted.

Elias rolled his eyes. "That idiot." He pointed his chin at Parker, who was at the center of the table while people practically gushed over him. He was obviously very popular. Ember found it disgusting. "He put irreversible powder on me."

"How?" Ember asked.

"In my shampoo," he said. "I didn't realize until it was too late."

So that must be why Parker had been in detention.

"The headmistress wouldn't entertain my many requests for a change of roommate," Elias said. Ember raised a brow. She didn't know they were roommates.

"I can't stand that obnoxious being," Elias said.

Ember side-eyed him. Elias turned to her with a frown. "What are you looking at?"

"Nothing," she said, shrugging. The last thing she needed was a fight with Elias, and he seemed to have quite a lot on his plate right now. Literally, the shimmery dust slid off his body and onto his food plate. Elias scowled at it as he walked away.

"What's up with him?" Chloe asked, joining Ember at one of the half-empty long tables.

"Parker put Irreversible Powder on him," Ember said, taking a bite of her stuffed sandwich. Thanks to the naturalists, Glofiara never ran out of food, and you could have a mix and match of anything that you liked to eat.

"Parker is the worst," Chloe said. "You would think him being different would make him sympathetic to others."

Ember watched as he waved around a hook at the tip of his amputated arm, pretending like he was the pirate Blackbeard, one of the most infamous remnants and a Water user.

"He's definitely obnoxious," Ember said.

Chloe's eyes flickered down to Ember's arms. "You can ask."

"Your scars..." Chloe trailed off.

Ember followed her gaze and shrugged. "I don't remember how I got them. They have been there as long as my memory goes."

"Your fire isn't supposed to hurt you, is it?" Chloe asked.

Ember paused. "I suppose." Her parents had just told her that she had been in an accident, and they never elaborated on that. And as hard as she tried, Ember remembered nothing.

"Maybe something fell on me," she mused.

"I'm glad you're okay," Chloe said.

"The scars don't hurt," Ember said. "But the stares used to bother me; that's why, when I was younger, I never took my jacket off."

"And now?"

"I simply don't care," Ember said with a shrug.

"I think I am the opposite," Chloe said. "I care a lot, which ends up hurting me."

"We are different," Ember agreed. "But it's not necessarily a bad thing." They were far from being friends, but at least they had good rapport as roommates.

"I like your hair," Chloe said. "I think it's very cool, especially with the blue tips. How did your parents let you dye it?"

"They didn't," Ember said, twirling a strand. "They were too busy dealing with evil sorcerers and Chupacabras to care." Her parents hadn't contacted her since the second day, and Ember supposed that they were already off on their new mission. Summer sometimes called to check up on her, but Ember rarely picked up. Her comm-device was inundated with messages from her older sister, but she didn't bother reading about the cool new thing Summer was doing while Ember couldn't even produce a stable flame for more than a few seconds.

The next day, Nadie wanted them to do a pair experiment. She separated the class into groups of twos and had them sit next to each other. Ember was unfortunately paired with...Elias, of all people.

She groaned under her breath.

"I heard that," Elias said. "I'm not very happy about the arrangement either, you know."

"Let's be honest, you don't like me, and I'm—well, not good with people," Ember said. "So I don't want to start a fight or whatever."

Elias frowned. "It's not that I don't like you. It's just that this country, language, culture, and everything else is a big adjustment for me."

Ember blinked. She hadn't thought of that. Before she could say anything else, Nadie called the class to attention. "Alright, everybody, I want you to turn to your partner and let yourself attune to their energy. I know it's going to sound weird at first, but I swear it works. When remnants are posted in the human world, they're most often put there in pairs, and everybody has to act like a team to get the job done. Is that clear?"

"This is ridiculous," Elias said. "What, am I supposed to let you fry my fingerprints off?"

Ember laughed. She looked around the class. A few of the students were grasping each other's hands, trying to concentrate, but mostly it felt like they were doing it to get Nadie off their backs.

Ember held out a hand to Elias. "Let's not make things difficult for each other and get this over with, okay?"

Elias stared at her uncomfortably. "I'm not sure about that."

"Why not?"

"B-because," Elias said. "All of this is still pretty new to me."

Ember understood what he meant. This wasn't his culture or custom. "Would it be better if I wear gloves?"

"Maybe?" Elias said shyly. "You can do that?"

"Sure," Ember said. She fished the silk gloves that her parents had gifted her after the test of age. She had never felt the need to wear them until now, but only because she didn't want to make Elias uncomfortable.

After she wore the gloves, she held her palms out, and Elias put his over hers. Nothing happened. It was just plain awkward.

"How long are we supposed to keep doing this?" Ember asked. She wanted to laugh at the silliness of it.

"Until class ends. That's another—what, thirty minutes?"

Ember suppressed a laugh. "We're going to get cramps by the end of it."

"What do you suppose we are going to tell Nadie we learned?" Elias said.

"Team spirit?" Ember suggested. A ghost of a smile tugged on Elias' lips. Just as suddenly, his eyes rolled into the back of his head, and his grip on her tightened, almost unbearably.

"Elias," Ember hissed. "You're hurting me."

And then she was transported into a vast space of unending darkness. Everything seemed to close in on her, slowly stifling her breath. Time rolled ahead patiently and unbearably slow.

A dark figure crouched on the floor, drawing a line across four others. There were hundreds of the markings, covering every surface in sight. These were days that had passed since this person was trapped in here.

Ember blinked, trying to make sense of where she was. It seemed like a prison cell. A rattling sound began, and the kneeling figure looked up. "Finally," he growled, his voice unlike anything she had heard before. It was like humanity had been slowly leached out of him until only rage remained. "My time has come."

A faint light pulsed in the distance, growing brighter and brighter until someone shook Ember awake. She blinked her eyes open as Elias and Nadie both stared at her worriedly.

"Ember, are you okay?"

Ember sat up groggily, touching her forehead. "I'm fine, but—" What had she seen? She was unable to make heads or tails out of it, and the images were slowly slipping out of her grasp.

"I'm sorry," Elias whispered. "It happens to me sometimes. I just lose it and bad things happen."

"It's fine, Elias," Nadie reassured him. "You're a clairvoyant, so it was probably just a vision. You're okay, right, Ember?"

Ember nodded. She knew dragging the incident out would only get Elias into further trouble.

"Do you remember what you saw?" Nadie asked.

"No," Ember said, still puzzled. "No idea."

Chapter Ten

THE FIVE EYES

The next day, early on Sunday morning, Ember was regretting Chloe dragging her out of bed at an unholy hour to take her down to the temple.

"Come on," Chloe said. "You always miss the morning prayers."

"That's because I know that Ethilenne would want me to get a good sleep rather than hear someone drone on about her life," Ember said.

Cloe frowned. "Is that what you think we do?"

Ember didn't reply and followed her into a small sandstone structure that was attached to the main school building. It opened up to an arching doorway smaller than the one at the main entrance but made of similar oakwood. The pews were filled to the brim with people, and there was a distinct hum in the air as people sang their prayers to Mother Ethilenne– also known as the original witch or Ancient One.

A copper statue of Ethilenne stood at the end of the aisle. Her eyes were open and her palms were facing out. Chloe gestured to Ember to sit down on one of the empty pews.

Ember's parents were always too busy for religion, and it wasn't really considered an important part of life. Nowadays, the community leaned towards the scientific aspect of ether magic rather than the spiritual.

Chloe waited until the rest of the temple emptied before making her way to the altar of Ethilenne. Ember followed her, staring up at the statue of the Veiled Lady. The lower part of her face was covered by a veil, while her eyes were open, her hair flowing behind. There was another eye between her brows, and two others on her palms.

"Why are there five eyes?" Ember thought aloud.

"The four eyes represent the five aspects of magic," said a voice behind them. Ember whirled on her heel. Headmistress Kinnera stood behind them. Like Elias usually was, she was dressed in all black. "Elemental, physical, natural, spiritual, and the fourth one—darkness."

A shiver shot down Ember's spine. "Darkness?"

"It's said to be a corrupt form of magic. It exists amongst us even though many people would choose to ignore it. Maybe that's why we let Mallorus be as powerful as he eventually became. Darkness exists in all of us, just as light does, and it all comes from Ethilenne."

"How so?" Chloe asked.

"After Ethilenne's brothers—Timonus, or time, and Spanithum, or space, as we call it in Science, betrayed her, she banished them both, but before that happened, the stolen power became corrupted, and it was unleashed into the world to become a sentient being of its own. That is the Darkness."

"Is Mallorus the Darkness?" Ember couldn't help but ask.

"I don't know, but he was certainly influenced by it," the headmistress replied.

"I don't really believe in myths. I'm more of a Sci-Magi girl," said Ember decidedly. Religion was for superstitious people, and she wasn't one of them.

"Certainly, but I've heard otherwise. It seems that you lack interest in most of your classes, including the Physical and Botanical aspects of Sci-Magi that you're taking this semester."

"It's just everything is very new to me," Ember said.

"So it is for the rest of the students," Kinnera countered.

"I'm sure I'll catch up soon," Ember said with a tight smile on her face.

"Indeed," Headmistress Kinnera said. "Are you familiar with the myth of Spanithum?"

"I've heard of him," Chloe said.

"Then you must have also heard what they say about him. Some say that he managed to hide a part of the power he stole, and it lives in the Chaos and is passed down through the remnants."

"Guess you learn new things every day," Ember said.

"Ether in Science or Ethilenne in religion, they're both two sides of the same coin," Headmistress Kinnera said. With a smirk, she walked away.

"She really hates us," Ember remarked. She had all but said that the remnants had stolen magic.

"I don't like her," Chloe said. "But I wonder why she chose to be the headmistress if she really doesn't like us."

"Maybe she wanted to torture us," Ember said. "Come on, let's get out of here."

Instead of heading upstairs, the two girls decided to take advantage of the bright day and head out into the open grounds. While they were walking, Ember spotted Nadie coming from the other side. She waved at her, but Nadie didn't seem to notice or acknowledge her. She had a distracted look on her face, and even her hair was a mess. She hurried away quickly in another direction, and Ember barely caught a glance at the leather-bound diary she was holding under her arm.

"That's weird," Ember said.

"Maybe she was just in a hurry," Chloe said.

"Maybe," Ember echoed.

The next morning, the girls were yet again late to class, but as it turned out, it didn't really matter. They were stopped by Mother Irene as they navigated to the other side of the campus to their first class.

"Where do you think you're going?"

"To our class, Facing History—oh, no, it's Cartography," Chloe said, stumbling on her own words.

"You can't even get your classes right and you're five minutes late," Irene said. "But that doesn't matter. Classes are canceled for today. You are to report to the Main Hall."

"Why?" Ember asked.

Mother Irene scowled at her. "You're a curious one, aren't you? Did Professor Owsmann manage to tame you yet? You've been keeping her hands rather full. Frankly, I don't know why she bothers with you lot."

Ember flushed. Was that true? Did Nadie think her company was a burden?

"Go now," Mother Irene said, her voice practically bellowing. Chloe tugged on Ember's sleeves to drag her away.

"Don't listen to her. She's mean, just like the Headmistress," Chloe said, her face darkening. "What do you think is going on in the Main Hall?"

"I have no idea," Ember said. "But I suppose we will find out soon enough."

The two of them made their way back to the Main Hall. By the time they arrived, it was already filled up. Today, there weren't just the first-years present but the upperclassmen as well. They were differentiated by the color of the patches on their blazers—blue and yellow for first year, green and white for second year, red and black for third year, orange and black for fourth, purple and silver for fifth, and black and gold for the graduating class. The remnants weren't allowed to wear mantles like full-fledged magi.

Ember and Chloe made sure that they were sitting with their classmates.

"What do you think is going on?" one of them asked.

"Maybe someone tried to start a fire in one of the Sci-Magi labs," Clarisse said, loud enough for Ember to hear. When Ember looked up, Clarisse was smirking at her. Next to her, Parker had an odd smile of his own. Ember remembered that he knew about her secret—or at least a part of it. She wondered if he had told Clarisse about it and she, in return, had told him about Ember's little accident during the test of age.

Ember was distracted when Headmistress Kinnera appeared on the dais. As usual, she was followed by the rest of the teachers—except two. Nadie was missing, and just as Ember began to wonder about Professor Detteo, he rushed in, wiping the sweat off his forehead as if he had been running. Headmistress Kinnera frowned at him as he walked up to the platform. He stood next to Professor Burke, who whispered something in his ear before Detteo nodded.

Headmistress Kinnera turned to face the crowd. "Students, I called this session because I'm aware of the rumors that are being spread around, the whispers that aren't doing anyone any good but causing rampant fear. I want to address all of that so you know the truth of the matter. I do not want to keep this from you."

The entire amphitheater seemed to hold their breath in anticipation.

"We have received terrible news this morning. The dark sorcerer Mallorus escaped his prison at Thanatos the night before last."

Everyone gasped in unison, almost as if it were an orchestra.

The headmistress continued. "Thanatos is not just any prison; it's guarded by the fabric of space and time itself, and Mallorus managed to rip through a tiny part of it."

Ember sucked in a breath. Since her parents had defeated him twenty years ago, she'd always thought of him as any other villain that was defeated by her parents, as opposed to his infallible image held by the rest of the community. But now Ember began to think otherwise. He had done the impossible, after all.

"Nobody knows about his whereabouts since, but a team of white sorcerers and diviners have been sent to investigate and I hope that we will have some answers soon."

Headmistress Kinnera paused while the entire amphitheater broke into frantic whispers, an air of unease making its way through the crowd. "You need not be alarmed, children. I'm certain that Mallorus will be appropriately dealt with. He has no business here, so he likely wouldn't try to harm us right away. But for your protection, a group of warlocks will be arriving tomorrow. They will guard our borders and you, so long as you cooperate. That's all I needed to say."

The amphitheater buzzed with curiosity and nervous ramblings as people discussed Mallorus and what his escape meant for the future of the community. Most of the young students weren't old enough to remember Mallorus's reign of terror.

"I heard once he put an entire hall of people to sleep and they never woke up again," someone was saying.

"Anybody who rose against him was punished severely. They lost a hand, or a leg, or his favorite—the head," Clarisse said. A few of the girls surrounding her squealed in horror as they ran away. Clarisse chuckled in satisfaction.

Ember shook her head in disgust. They were using people's fear for their own amusement. Beside Ember, Chloe shivered, her hands wrapped around herself. "I'm scared, Ember."

"You heard what the Headmistress said, right? Mallorus is not coming this way. We are remnants; we aren't of any real use to him. He'll probably go after the Society first."

Chloe stopped walking. "Aren't you worried about your parents?"

The truth was, Ember was indeed scared. Her parents were the ones who had locked Mallorus away. There had been seven of them, of all orders, and the team was led by the Pearsons. If somebody had stuck her in a timeless prison, she would come after her jailers as soon as she could.

"They're in Peru. They haven't been able to call me since, and I suppose even Mallorus might have a little trouble finding them."

"Where do you think he could be hiding?" Chloe said.

"Maybe look behind your curtains first," Parker said, sneaking up from behind them and making a ghostly sound. Chloe shrieked and almost head-butted him.

"He's still alive, idiot," Ember said, glaring at him.

"Sure," Parker said, rolling his eyes. He walked ahead of them while Ember made a face.

"You know, when I first came in here, before Orientation, he was actually nice to me," said Chloe.

"Really?" Ember said, hardly believing it.

"My foster sister dropped me off because she was running late. Parker helped me with my bags," she said. "He seemed very sweet."

"Well, he's definitely the opposite," Ember said distractedly. She was searching for Nadie, but she was nowhere to be found. "Hey, by any chance, did you spot Nadie before?"

Chloe shook her head. "No, she wasn't up on the dais with the other professors. Maybe she is busy."

"The headmistress just told us that the evilest wizard in our history just broke out of an unbreakable prison. What could be more important than that?" Ember wondered.

"We'll probably see her later," Chloe assured her.

But she was wrong, because Nadie was nowhere to be seen for the rest of the day. Ember made two trips to her locked office, and the next day, Nadie never showed up for Creativity class.

Ember couldn't get it out of her mind. Nadie wouldn't just disappear into thin air for no reason. She hadn't even told Ember that she was leaving. Ember thought back to the time she had seen her on the lawn, yesterday. She had appeared almost distracted, so much so that she didn't even notice Ember.

Ember was lost in her thoughts on the way back from Creativity class when she spotted Headmistress Kinnera walking down a flight of stairs. She had a comm-device in her hand, into which she was speaking urgently. As soon as she put it away, Ember followed her.

"Headmistress," she called. "Headmistress Kinnera. There's something I wanted to talk to you about."

Kinnera peered down at her. She was so impossibly tall that she towered over Ember. "Yes?"

"It's about Professor Owsmann. She didn't teach our class today."

"Excuse me?"

"And she's nowhere to be seen," Ember said frantically. She expected the headmistress to show concern, anything but the apathy that was written on her face. She regarded Ember like a fly she wanted to swat away.

"Professor Owsmann is a warlock," she said impassively. "She can handle herself, Miss Pearson. I advise you to look after yourself."

"But she has disappeared and no one is looking—"

"There is nothing," Kinnera said, "and I mean nothing, more important for me than to make sure everyone at Glofiara is safe and sound. Nadie has a habit of helping people out. She must have stepped out for a day or two."

"But—"

"All my resources are being directed towards the safety of my students and making sure the Society has my cooperation while we find and return the dark sorcerer to his prison. If you have any problem with that, you may take it up with your parents."

Ember stared at the headmistress with dismay. Headmistress Kinnera was right. Ember didn't have any proof that Nadie was in trouble, but her heart said otherwise. She wouldn't just leave without talking to her.

"Headmistress, I really—"

"But, since you insist, I'll have someone look into it," she said. "Would that be to your satisfaction, Miss Pearson?"

Ember nodded, not knowing what else to say. The headmistress's dislike for her was palpable.

Ember trudged back to her room dejectedly. Chloe sat up on her bed when she entered. "Did you find anything?"

Ember shook her head. "The headmistress didn't take me seriously. She said she would have someone look into it, but I think she just said that to get me off her back."

Chloe furrowed her brow. "I think we should trust the adults. I'm sure the headmistress is doing everything she can to make sure everyone is safe."

"Maybe she is," Ember said, "but I can't just wait around for the adults to do something. I'm going to do everything *I* can to find Nadie."

Chapter Eleven

REVENGE

Three days went by, but there was no sign of Nadie. It seemed that Ember was the only one concerned about her disappearance.

"Come on," Chloe said. "You can't just sit in here and sulk. We should go out and enjoy the sun. You're starting to turn as pale as a vampire."

"Fine," Ember said reluctantly. A few other students seemed to have the same idea. They were camped out on the lawn, basking in the sun, and had picnic baskets laid out in front of them. It was almost as if Mallorus had never escaped his prison.

Ember laid back, listening to music from her favorite band, Witch and the Cursed Hand. They were alternative rock with pop tones. Ember loved them, mostly because of how vocal they had been for the cause of remnants.

Chloe sat beside her, taking shots of the lawn and the forest that loomed in the distance. She stood up slowly and started backing away while she said, "It's a sunny day in Glofiara, but is it the beginning of our doom?"

"Are you trying to be like one of those gossip reporters on EtherTele?" Ember asked, chuckling. Someone shrieked nearby, and Ember's smile faded. Chloe had accidentally collided with Clarisse while she was taking the shot.

"You freak," Clarisse said, shoving Chloe to the ground.

Ember scowled as she ran up to them. "What is your problem?"

"My problem?" Clarisse said, her high-pitched voice making Ember cringe. "This freak ruined my shoes. I should break her little human gadget."

"If you do that," Ember said quietly, "I'll burn your shoes and throw them into the forest and wish you good luck finding them."

Clarisse fumed. Instead of saying anything to Ember, she addressed Chloe, who was still on the ground. "Careful, she might accidentally burn you." With a huff, she left.

Ember knelt on the ground beside Chloe. "You okay?"

"I'm fine," Chloe said, brushing a hand down her skirt. "I swear I almost scraped my knee on a coin though."

"Coin?" Ember asked.

"This," Chloe said, pulling the object out from under her. It wasn't a coin at all, but an ornate key. It shone faintly under the sun. And it looked familiar.

"Wait," Ember said, trying to place it. "I have seen this key before. This is the key to Nadie's office!"

"What's it doing on the lawn?" Chloe said, frowning down at it. "Wouldn't she need it?"

Ember looked around, realizing that they were only a couple of hundred feet away from the forest. "Do you think she went in there?"

"That's ridiculous," Chloe said. "Why would she go into the forest? We're forbidden to do so."

Ember stared down at the key. "There's only one way to find out."

"Are you thinking the same thing I'm thinking?" Chloe said.

Ember nodded. "I think so."

"Okay, then we should give the key to Headmistress Kinnera," Chloe said. "She'll know what to do with it."

Ember shook her head. "That wasn't what I was thinking at all. We should go into her office. Professor Patel has a logbook where she keeps accounts of her daily activities; maybe Nadie has one too."

"How do you know that?"

"It's a long story," Ember said patiently. "The point is that we have the key, and it would be a crime not to do anything about it. Kinnera couldn't care less about Nadie's disappearance. She's only focused on Mallorus."

"Don't mention him," Chloe said urgently, looking around.

"Okay, fine, I won't," Ember said, getting to her feet. "But we must find out if Nadie is okay. If she left the school for a few days, she would have noted that in her logbook."

"Okay," Chloe said. "But we must be careful."

"Chloe," Ember said. "It's better if I go there alone. I don't want you to get into any trouble."

"And what about you?"

"I'll be fine," Ember said with a confidence she didn't actually feel.

Fifteen minutes later, Ember found herself in the empty corridor. The Creativity classroom was just down the end of the hallway. She tiptoed there, waiting to make sure that the coast was clear before making her way inside. It was odd to go up there when it was so eerily quiet, instead of filled with students talking over each other.

Ember waited with bated breath as she pushed the key into the lock. The lock clicked and the door opened with a creak. She stared in disbelief. A part of her had thought that she had the wrong key, but she finally had access to Nadie's office.

At first, she didn't quite know what to do. Considering Headmistress Kinnera's weird beef with her, Ember wouldn't be surprised if she used this incident to expel her. Ember walked to Nadie's table. It was cluttered with odd books, talismans, feathers, and charms, amongst other things. Ember had the feeling that Nadie wasn't the most organized person.

She finally found what she was looking for—a leather bound notebook with Nadie's name printed on the front. The pages had grown sticky and brown over time. She flipped to the last updated page and found an odd note:

Injured at the Menagerie. Must find it.

Ember frowned to herself. Was Nadie concerned about an injured animal down at the Menagerie? And what was she even hoping to find? There was a list of botanical ingredients written below it. Ember didn't recognize any of the names. The note looked like it was hurriedly written, barely legible, and had today's date.

She was pondering what it could mean when the door opened and Elias walked in. The two stared at each other, first in confusion, and then with dawning horror.

"What are you doing here?" Ember cried at the same time Elias said, "How did you get in here?"

The two fell silent, eyeing each other with mutual distrust. Ember knew that Elias was a tattler. It wouldn't take him two minutes to go to the headmistress.

"Nadie gave me the key to her office. She wanted me to check up on something," Ember said.

"Why don't I believe you?" Elias asked, folding his arms over his chest. "Besides, I haven't seen Professor Owsmann since the day before yesterday."

"She was here recently," Ember said. *If the note is any indication*, she thought. She kept that part to herself.

Elias frowned at her before looking down at her hands. "Have you been reading her diary?"

"It's just a logbook," Ember said defensively.

"Right," Elias said sarcastically.

"If you report me, you'll get into trouble too," Ember said, grasping at straws. "I know you don't want this to tarnish your perfect reputation."

Elias's lips pursed into a thin line. "Were you in here stealing?"

"No," Ember said, but the logbook in her hand gave her away. "I swear, it's not what it looks like."

"I don't care why you are here as long as you help me," Elias said impatiently.

"Wait, what?" Ember said, blinking in shock.

"I need to take revenge on Parker for what he did to me," Elias said. The odd shimmer on his body had yet to fade away. "I'm not going to let his insolence go unanswered."

"Is that why you're here?" Ember asked, catching on.

Elias hesitated before nodding. "Nadie is the oddest person around. I was sure she would have something that would help me get back at Parker." He picked up a strange-looking orb from a nearby stash. "Maybe this will help."

"I don't think that's a good idea," Ember said hesitantly. "Besides, why would a teacher help you bully someone?"

"It's not bullying when he started it," Elias snapped. It was the first time Ember had seen him lose his temper.

"Are you going to help me or not?" he finally said.

"Fine," Ember said. It was still better than everybody finding out the truth. "I'll help you, but you have to keep my secret in turn."

The two made their way downstairs together. "What do you think happened to Nadie?" asked Elias.

"Headmistress Kinnera said that she was probably away helping someone."

"Is that why you were snooping around in her room?" Elias countered. He glanced sideways at Ember. "You don't trust the headmistress."

Ember bit her lip. "It's just that Mallorus has escaped, and Nadie has gone missing. What if—"

Elias laughed. He actually laughed. "You don't really think that Mallorus is here or that he kidnapped Nadie, do you?"

Ember hesitated, because that was exactly what she had thought.

"Oh my Ethilenne, you're not serious," Elias said. "What would a dark wizard even want with an eccentric school teacher who wears mismatched clothes? The answer is nothing, because he has better things to do."

"Pray, what things does he have?" Ember asked, scowling.

"Hello? He just escaped prison. He's probably out there hunting people who wronged him and—" Elias paused. In fact, he stopped walking altogether. "I'm sorry, Ember, I didn't think about..." He trailed off again.

"It's fine," Ember said with wavering confidence. She had been trying to contact her parents in Peru, but they were unreachable. They were probably fine, but she couldn't help but worry. "He's not strong enough to come after my parents. They have been at it all these years that he has been in jail."

"Right. So tell me, what's the plan for pranking Parker?" Elias said. "I'm sure with your colorful imagination you'll come up with something."

Ember flushed. "Hey, no need to make fun of me. It was just a thought."

"Come on," Elias said impatiently. "I need your help." Even though he didn't say it, the "or else" was clear. There was nothing keeping him from snitching on her.

"I don't know," Ember said honestly. She had pranked her sister before but knew Parker would be a harder catch. Besides, she was distracted by Nadie's disappearance. Elias was right. Her reasoning might be totally off, but it was still odd that Nadie had left without saying anything. Ember had thought that they were making good progress together when it came to containing her powers. What would happen now? Was Nadie able to manage handing off the vial to Professor Detteo before she left? Did that even matter now that she was gone? Suddenly, Ember had a vision of her dream studying at Zanith slowly fading away until it was just a distant, hazy picture, quickly smudged by time.

And then there was Mallorus. The adults could probably deal with him, but Ember couldn't stop thinking of the records that Summer and she had spent entire summers poring over. Her parents never threw away any of their investigative files, and for Mallorus, they had a stack of those. Ember remembered how her spine had tingled every time she had read about one of his gruesome acts. Even though Mallorus was gone long before she could even walk or speak, to Ember he had always seemed like a living, breathing thing, as opposed to the myth that most children her age thought. She could almost feel his invisible fingers squeezing her neck, making it impossible to breathe.

Probably for the first time since she had heard it, the implication of his escape began to dawn on Ember. Would history repeat itself? Would someone—maybe her parents—be able to stop him before he regained his powers?

"We need to do something that really takes him by surprise," Elias said, bringing her back to the present. "Kaboom."

"Excuse me?" Ember said.

"For Parker, I mean. We need to catch him off guard."

"You aren't thinking of explosives, are you?" Ember said, raising a brow. They turned the corner and came face-to-face with someone very familiar.

"Summer?" Ember squeaked. Her sister was the last person she had expected to see at Glofiara. Summer looked pretty as ever, her shimmery blond hair tucked away in a tight braid. She was wearing gray slacks paired with a deep red tunic, the same outfit Ember had noticed over the comm-call. That was probably her apprentice uniform. Ember quickly hid the logbook behind her back.

"I heard someone say something about explosives," Summer said suspiciously before her gaze fell to Elias. "I didn't know you were friends with a pixie."

"I'm not a pixie," Elias said indignantly.

Ember was sweating. If Summer discovered the logbook in her custody, everything would be over.

"The pixie can speak human?" Summer asked, her brows raised.

"For the last time, I'm not a pixie," Elias said, folding his arms over his chest, a deepening scowl on his face.

"This is Elias," Ember said hastily before Elias started to argue with her sister and possibly ruin everything. "Someone put Irreversible Powder on him, and that's why he looks that way."

Elias finally seemed to realize who they were talking to. "Summer Pearson," he said almost breathlessly.

Ember rolled her eyes while her sister tossed her hair dramatically. Summer's hawk-like gaze fell on Ember again, who gulped visibly. There was little that she could hide from her. In the next moment, her arms felt lighter. She glanced sideways at Elias who winked at her. He had carefully extracted the logbook from her hands.

"Do you have something behind your back?"

Ember brought her hands forward. "Nope, look for yourself."

Summer grumbled under her breath. "Anyway, you shouldn't be out here alone."

"Why not?" Ember asked. "And who made you the boss of me?"

"Actually, little sister," Summer said, smirking at her. She draped a hand over her shoulder and started to walk forward. "I'm glad you brought that up. I've been posted at Glofiara as one of the protective agents."

"Wait, you're here to guard us against Mallorus?" Ember asked. "But you're not even done with your training yet."

"I'm an apprentice," Summer said with a slight sniff. "I have all the required tools and knowledge I need."

Ember shook her head. "So they sent the new recruits to Glofiara. I guess it's not like this place is in real trouble. Mallorus would rather be somewhere he has something to gain, not at a school where someone might accidentally freeze him to death or make his head explode."

Summer frowned. "You know those are all remnant stereotypes that I don't believe in."

"Oh?" Ember said. "Wake up, Summer. You know why I'm here." *You were complicit in sending me away,* Ember wanted to say.

"You're still mad at me?" Summer said, not quite meeting her gaze.

"Umm, let me see, you lied to me so that I agreed with you like the little sheep I am, and then you abandoned me here where nothing good was going to happen to me."

Summer looked taken aback. "That's not true."

"It's fine," Ember said, finding a semblance of patience. "I know you'd rather be at Zanith protecting its gifted children or whatever. Glofiara has as much chance of being attacked as the sun rising from the west."

"Don't be so sure about that," Summer said. "Mallorus is weak, so he's probably looking for support. He may try to recruit remnants with unstable power to use as a weapon against the Society."

Ember stiffened. Elias had started inching away from them. "Yeah, you're probably right. I better go," Ember said, cutting her sister off. "We're late for dinner."

Elias walked off with the logbook, and before Ember could follow him, her sister tugged on her arm. Summer hesitated before finally saying, "Ember, listen, have you heard from our parents?"

Ember shook her head. A part of her was hoping that they had at least contacted Summer. "They're not back from Peru yet?"

Summer shook her head. "Nobody has heard from them in three days. People are worried."

"I'm sure they'll call you when they finally have a signal," Ember said with a smile. "You are, after all, their favorite daughter." But at the back of her mind, Ember couldn't help but think something was off, and that something worse was on its way.

Chapter Twelve

A PESKY DOTTED CHIMERA

Chloe was standing by their room door. Even Toasty the toad was on her shoulder, waiting to greet her. Ember didn't let it bother her how well the two of them got along.

"So," Chloe said. "What did you find out?"

Ember looked down at her arms and remembered that the logbook had remained with Elias.

"I had to get rid of Nadie's logbook for now. My sister distracted me," Ember said.

"Wait," Chloe said, her brows furrowed. "I'm so confused—you found a logbook? Where did you hide it? And why is your sister here?"

Ember caught Chloe up to everything that had happened. "I did find something odd in her logbook. It was her last entry, and Nadie wrote about wanting to find a wounded animal and then a list of botanical ingredients below it."

Chloe's eyes widened. "What does it mean?"

Ember shook her head. "I won't know until I get the logbook back. But get this—the last entry was for today's date."

Chloe's eyes widened. "So she disappeared in the last twenty-four hours? After Mallorus got out?"

"Correct," Ember said. "But if that's the case, why didn't we see her in the last two days?"

Both the girls fell silent.

"But wait, where exactly is the logbook?" Chloe asked before checking herself. She cleared her throat. "I mean, if you want me to see it."

"Chloe—" Ember said. "Of course I want you to see it. You found the key, after all. In fact, let's join forces. We can look for Nadie together, if that's what you want...."

Chloe's smile was so wide Ember's insides squeezed. She nodded vigorously.

"So where is it?"

"That's the thing. Elias took it to hide from my sister. If Summer saw it, we both would have been in big trouble. I guess we'll just wait until tomorrow."

The next morning, Ember slid into the empty table beside Elias. Chloe followed her.

"Why did you steal Professor Owsmann's logbook?" Elias asked.

"Not so loudly," Ember hissed. "People might hear us."

"Don't worry," he said. "It's back in my dorm tower. I saw the little note she had written at the back."

"Really?" Ember asked. She had hoped he would do that. "And what did you gather from that exactly?"

Elias smirked at her. "Not so fast, Pearson. First, you'll tell me your plans for pranking Parker."

"I'll set your food on fire," Ember said calmly. "Don't test me."

Elias scowled. "That's why I hate working with elementals. You people are way too emotional."

"If you're calling me unstable—"

"I'm not saying that," Elias said, rolling his eyes.

"Just tell me what you found."

"Very well. She had a list of botanical ingredients. I identified four of them."

"Just four?"

"Yes," Elias said, looking offended. "How many did you identify?"

"You had the logbook, I didn't," Ember pointed out.

Elias sniffed rather snootily. "Most of them are rare ingredients not easily found just anywhere."

"Would they be found, say, hypothetically, in the forest?" Ember asked.

Elias nodded. "Possibly," he said. "The forest is said to contain a treasure trove of ancient herbs. In fact, about fifty years ago, a botanist started to classify his findings that would have been revolutionary for his generation."

"What happened?" Chloe asked.

Elias looked at her somberly. "He never returned. One night, they say they heard his screams."

Ember felt a shiver pass down her spine. "These are all tales spun to keep us out of there. There is one about an Ancient One hiding in the forest, isn't there?"

"Are you sure about that?" Elias asked.

"I think that Nadie went into the forest to find those ingredients for the injured animal," Ember said. "Whatever it was."

"But you don't know for sure," Elias pointed out. "It's a hypothesis, and putting your life on the line for something not yet proven is nothing short of insanity."

"Maybe," Ember said. Elias was thinking logically; Ember wasn't. She knew how kind-hearted Nadie was. She would definitely put her life on the line for an injured animal. "But we'll find out soon enough." Ember just needed to chart a way into the forest.

She pulled something from her pocket. It was a green orb as big as a golf ball. "Here," Ember said. "You'll need this."

"What is it?" Elias asked, frowning at it.

"It's a skunk bomb for Parker," Ember said. "It's something hunting warlocks use to track their targets. Stole it from my sister's bag." Ember had gone down to Summer's quarters early in the morning on the pretext of meeting her and, when she wasn't looking, simply snuck one out of her traveling bag. Ember was certain that she wouldn't even know it was gone, as she didn't have any actual need of it at Glofiara.

The three of them glanced at Parker, who was holding court with his friends. "Let's see how much his cronies can stand him after he starts smelling like ten dead skunks."

Elias chuckled. "Remind me never to cross you."

"Thank my sister for that," Ember said. As if summoned by her thoughts, Summer walked towards them.

"Hide that," Ember muttered under her breath just as Summer walked up to their table. Elias quickly shoved the logbook behind his back. Ember didn't exactly know how Summer would react if her sister found out that she had broken into a teacher's office and stolen something. Summer had always been a stickler for rules. One time when Ember was eight, she had accidentally burned down a tree in the backyard of their house in suburban Ohio. Her parents would have never noticed it if Summer hadn't tattled. According to Summer, it was all about the principles. She had no respect for the sister bond.

"Ember," Summer said, frowning at her. There was no way she could know yet.

"Yes?" Ember asked hesitantly.

"Our parents are here," Summer said. "Come on, let's meet them."

Ember glanced at Elias and Chloe before following her sister. She had changed into her purple mantle of warlock, and Ember couldn't help but feel a pang of jealousy at that. She may never have one of her own.

"Are you here alone?" Ember asked.

"No, two of my fellow apprentices are here with me," Summer explained. They stopped in front of the small courtyard that divided the school premises from the living quarters. Their parents were sitting on a courtyard bench. They had deep bags under their eyes, their hair was a mess, and they looked like they had been up for several days.

Ember forgot all about her misgivings. They were imperfect, but at the end of the day, they were still family. "Mom, Dad," Ember said, running to her parents.

Ember's mother ruffled her hair affectionately. "Kiddo, we missed you so much."

Ember crinkled her nose. "Why do you smell so bad? Did one of the skunk balls fall on you?"

Her father laughed, but it didn't reach his eyes like it usually did.

"Did you manage to find what you were looking for?" Summer asked. Their parents exchanged a glance with each other.

"Now that I think about it—why were you in Peru in the first place?" Ember asked, frowning.

"We ended up, um, chasing down a rather pesky dotted chimera," her mother said. "We were out of contact with the rest of the world because we were stuck deep inside the Amazon."

"Really? They sent you just for that?" Summer said. "Seems a job beneath your status. I thought you went because the locals had sighted a Chullachaqui?"

"Yeah, there was some mistake in the translation," her mother said.

George Pearson shook his head. Both of her parents shifted uncomfortably, almost as if they were trying to hide something. Summer was right. It felt strange that the Pearsons would be assigned to a low-level threat.

"No job is too big or small. The chimera gave us quite a chase, and we ended up someplace where even the comm-device stopped working. That's why it took us so long to come."

"So what exactly is going on with Mallorus?" Ember asked.

"We haven't gone by the Conservation Society yet; we thought we should drop in and check on you first," George said. He stood and walked to Summer, fiercely engulfing her in a hug. "I missed you. Both of you."

Ember almost snorted. He had said the latter almost absentmindedly, as if Ember weren't really there. Ember's dad went in for a hug, but after an awkward shuffle, she quickly moved out of his grasp. She had never felt comfortable hugging her parents. Affection was mostly reserved for Summer while she won accolades or did whatever else she was perfect at.

Her father frowned as if he were just noticing that Ember never hugged him back.

"Children, you must already be aware of what happened," Rosetta Pearson said.

Summer nodded. "That's the reason I'm here—Mallorus got out."

Her parents exchanged a solemn look. "But from what we heard from our sources inside the Society, he didn't escape alone; he was broken out of there."

Ember and Summer gasped in unison. "Oh my Ethilenne, who could it be?"

"We don't know yet," Rosetta said, shaking her head. "But when he was at the height of his influence, he had plenty of people devoted to his cause. It might have been one of them."

"But isn't the prison of Thanatos unbreakable?" Summer pointed out. "Nobody else has gotten out before. They say you need the magic of the..."

"The Ancient Ones," George finished. "Yes, but they haven't been around for a long time. Maybe things have changed."

Ember remembered what Nadie had told her about there being more remnants than ever. Maybe there was more to it than she'd assumed before.

"The Ancient Ones aren't real," Ember said.

"They were—once upon a time," Summer said.

"Since when do you believe in Theology?" Ember countered.

"They really get into this stuff at—" She paused, and Ember realized what she was about to say.

"Zanith," Ember finished. Summer nodded.

"Religion and Magi-science are interrelated," her mother agreed. "Although I don't believe much in the former."

"There must be some rational explanation to what happened," George said, ever the rational. "Of course an Ancient One didn't help Mallorus break out."

Ember and Summer both laughed despite themselves.

George sobered quickly. He glanced at his two daughters. "You have to be very careful. We don't know what he's plotting, or what his next move could be. Mallorus is dangerous."

Ember swallowed hard before nodding. Her gaze fell to the tall, unyielding forest in the distance. She didn't know what lay beyond that, but if she hoped to rescue Nadie, she would have to find out.

"You keep saying that, but you haven't actually told us why that is," Ember suddenly said.

Her parents blinked. "What?"

"What makes Mallorus so dangerous? How did he become that way?" Ember said.

They were quiet for a few moments, and Ember thought that they weren't going to say anything. They always shut down when anything about Mallorus came up. Finally, her mom said, "The reason we never told you about him is because we didn't want you to go through or recount the trauma."

"You knew him, before he became...whatever he is?" Ember said.

"Yes," her dad said, lost in thought. "He wasn't always that way."

"But then—"

"You girls are safe here," George said. "He's not coming here. The last known sources put him somewhere in Asia. That's all you need to know. Now, if you girls will excuse us, we need to meet with Headmistress Kinnera." They walked out of the courtyard, disappearing into one of the cobble-stoned hallways.

"Why do they never tell us?" Ember said.

"Did you see the look on their faces?" Summer said. "Whatever they went through must be really traumatic, and the reason nobody talks about Mallorus or his powers anymore is because the Society has sworn everybody involved to secrecy."

"I wonder why that is," Ember said. "Wouldn't we be better prepared if we knew what we were up against?"

Summer laughed. "You want to go up against Mallorus?"

Ember scowled. "Why? What's wrong with that?"

Summer patted Ember's head. She shook out of her grip and stepped away. "Good luck with that, little sister."

"Don't patronize me."

"You're better off thinking about your homework than Mallorus. Let the adults deal with the big problems."

"I suppose you consider yourself as one, as well?"

Summer tossed her hair behind her back. "Well, I'm eighteen, so yeah, pretty much."

As Ember stood there with her sister, her comm-device buzzed with a flurry of incoming messages.

Ew, Parker stinks!

Someone send him to a nurse.

I can't stand it. He smells like a thousand dead skunks.

Ember smiled to herself, a deep rumbling satisfaction in her. Parker deserved what he got.

"What are you smiling at?" Summer asked, frowning.

"Nothing," Ember said. Summer might underestimate her, but once she put her mind to something, she made sure she got it done. That was why Ember knew that she was going to find Nadie, and she was going to bring her home.

Chapter Thirteen

THE MENAGERIE

The plan consisted of several steps that Chloe and Ember concocted later that night. The first—and obvious—step was to find out more about the injured animal. The next day after they were done with their classes, Chloe and Ember decided to go down to the Menagerie—a.k.a. the place where all the trouble probably began. She needed to find Nadie, but before that, she had to retrace all her steps. That's what any good investigator would do. In fact, she already had a checklist made.

1. *Investigate the Menagerie for the injured animal.*

2. *Find out all about the plants and herbs that Nadie mentioned in her logbook.*

3. *Find out who saw Nadie last before she disappeared.*

"Do you mind if I keep my recorder rolling?" Chloe asked.

Ember shot her an amused glance. "Sure, but why?"

"I'm trying to cover all the evidence we gather for a documentary about Nadie's disappearance," Chloe said. Ember could tell from her solemn voice that she wasn't joking. "Maybe if Headmistress Kinnera sees it, she might change her mind."

"I doubt that," Ember said. "But we can try."

Together the two girls made their way across the field to the Menagerie. The thick plush grass gave way to a small dirt road that snaked all the way down to the enclosure. It was only a few hundred feet to the forest, and despite herself, Ember felt a shiver climb down her spine. She shuddered to think about what lay beyond the dense line of trees.

The Menagerie was a sprawling enclosure at the edge of the forest that housed a myriad of animals. It had a chain-link fence built around a twelve-foot wall of thick wood, which made it impossible to peer inside. In the distance, there were distinct sounds of animal cries. Natural inlet water pipes were built in from the side, probably to feed the animals.

Ember pushed the heavy doors open and immediately the pungent smell of manure and animal greeted her.

Chloe pinched the bridge of her nose with her fingers. "Geez, this place stinks."

Ember couldn't agree more. There were large wooden enclosures on either side—mostly small furry animals locked away. Ember recognized a few of them, but most were exotic species she had never seen before.

"What exactly are we looking for?" Chloe asked.

"I guess we'll know when we see it," Ember said. Chloe nodded, her recorder out as she walked to each enclosure and took videos.

Ember wandered farther in with Chloe at her back. "That's strange," Chloe said. "There's nothing inside."

Chloe stood in front of one of the enclosures. Like the rest of them, it was made of mesh fire fencing that kept the animal inside. As she watched, a big furry animal charged towards the mesh fence.

"Look out!" Ember yelled just as Chloe turned around. The creature had its long fangs out, its large jaw coated with saliva. Chloe screamed and scrambled backward, her recorder dropping to the ground.

Ember kneeled beside her. "You okay?"

The large, amber-eyed creature continued to growl and paw at the ground as it fixed its beady eyes on Chloe.

"The Ottomaris can sense dark magic," said a voice behind them. It came from the last person Ember expected to see.

"What are you doing here, Parker?" she asked. He had an apron tied over his waist and large gum boots that were covered with mud and something else that Ember didn't want to identify. He carried a shovel in his hand.

He walked to the enclosure and beat on it with the shovel. The Ottomaris huffed before retreating into the darkness. "Bingo is usually nice. You must have spooked him," Parker said.

"Sure," Ember said sarcastically as she pulled Chloe up from the ground. She brushed the flecks of mud off her body.

"What did you say about dark magic?" Chloe asked.

"Don't listen to him," Ember said, narrowing her eyes. "He doesn't know what he's talking about."

"You're wrong about that," Parker said, his lips thinning. "I was just stating facts."

"Maybe this one time you've got it wrong, because hello—in case you're forgetting—I'm non-magic," Chloe said, pointing at herself. Ember expected him to say something sarcastic, but he didn't.

"I can't believe you named that vile creature Bingo," Ember said.

"I help out the Keeper sometimes," he said with a shrug as if it were the most natural answer.

Ember looked around as if to make a point. "You like spending your time here? In this dump?"

"Most of them are injured animals that have been brought in from distant lands for rehabilitation; others were born here and will be released into the wild once they are old enough," Parker said. "Animals are much kinder than human beings."

Ember snorted. "You're one to talk. Or did you change your mind after the...unfortunate incident you had yesterday?" She wrinkled her nose even though she couldn't really smell anything over the animals around her. There was a large keep where the animals were allowed to have free reign, but it did little to get the odor off their bodies.

Parker's eyes narrowed. He took a step towards Ember. "Don't think I'm a fool. I know Elias is the one who did it, but he isn't creative enough to have come up with it by himself. Surely he had some help. I also know that skunk bombs don't come around so easily."

"It's great that you're so clever," Ember said. She stood her ground.

"I've heard the warlocks use skunk bombs to trace the criminal they're staking. I also noticed that your sister was on campus."

"You can't prove anything."

Parker smirked. "Who said I want to prove anything? I like the way you think."

Ember looked at him warily. He was trying to get her defenses down and strike when she didn't expect it. "I don't trust you."

"With all due respect, Ember Pearson, I don't trust you either." The two continued to glare at each other.

"But I'm surprised you decided to help Elias."

Ember wasn't falling for his trap. "What's that supposed to mean?"

"He's such a stuck-up," Parker said.

Ember shook her head. "Have you looked at yourself? You're so mean to everyone around you."

"Guys," Chloe said. She looked uncomfortable. "Can you please not fight?"

"Fine," Parker finally said. "Why are you here?"

"We wanted to find some information," Ember said, looking around. Other than the Ottomaris, there were several other creatures—some no bigger than a house cat but with long fangs. Ember dimly remembered them being called Raokes. Then there were even smaller creatures, no bigger than sparrows, that flitted around in their cages, but Ember saw them for what they really were—pixies.

Chloe, who seemed to be fascinated by the pixies, stepped closer, but Ember put a hand on her shoulder to stop her. Even though they didn't look as dangerous or gargantuan as an Ottomaris, they were still pretty dangerous.

Next to the pixies were the Cachaews, the animals that had great camouflaging techniques. In the olden days, sorcerers used their skin to develop specialty invisible mantles or armors, but that had since been banned.

"Information about what?"

"About an injured animal," said Chloe, her recorder out and pointed at Parker.

"Are you recording me?" Parker asked.

"It's for the documentary," Chloe replied.

"What documentary?" Parker said, his head cocked.

Ember elbowed Chloe, but Parker caught on soon enough. "I see what's going on. You are looking for Nadie, aren't you? I wonder what the headmistress would say if she were to find out."

"You wouldn't," Ember warned.

"Why are you so obsessed with her anyway?" Parker said. Ember's ears turned red-hot.

"I'm not obsessed," she said. Nadie was the only one who could help her stabilize her power, paving her path to Zanith. Ember genuinely liked her as well. She was the first person to really see her. Only she couldn't say that to Parker.

"What do you plan to do next? Go into the Whispering Woods?" Parker chuckled.

This time the combined guilt on Ember and Chloe's faces gave them away.

Parker's smile faded. "You are planning that, aren't you? You're insane."

"Well, what does it matter to you?" Ember said. "Just give us our answer and we'll be on our way. We won't bother you."

"I don't know what you're talking about. There is no injured animal here."

"Perhaps we could talk to the Zoo-Keep," Ember said.

"He's not here," said Parker. "He went down to the Society headquarters, and he won't be back for at least a week. I'm volunteering in his absence. Well, it started as an extension of detention, but I'm quite enjoying it."

Ember knew he was lying. The alternative was to consider the fact that Parker could actually be nice.

Ember and Chloe glanced at each other. They weren't going to find any answers here.

"Are you sure?"

"Of course, I've been here every day. I would definitely have noticed an injured animal."

Ember walked to one of the empty keeps. "Why is nothing in there?"

Parker shrugged. "I don't know, maybe the Keeper moved the animal to Magi-Zoo or sent it off to another rehabilitation center before he left. Or maybe that's where he's gone. He didn't really give me any specifics."

"What do you mean?"

"He wasn't here yesterday, and I assumed that he had left for some important work. We don't exactly have the best resources here, and Glofiara has little to no funding. So, nope, no injured animals here,"

Parker said. "But he did leave a note saying he's due to return tomorrow, so I guess you can talk to him then."

"Hmph," Ember said, looking around. What if Professor Burke was missing as well? Would his disappearance have something to do with Nadie, or was Ember reading too much into it?

"Listen, you guys better leave. I've got a lot of stuff to do," Parker said.

"Well, that was a bust," Chloe said as soon as they left the Menagerie.

"Maybe," Ember said. "But I think something is amiss."

"You think Parker is lying?" Chloe asked.

"He might be trying to take revenge on me for helping Elias prank him, or maybe there is more to it."

"What do you mean?"

"Don't you think it's rather odd that the Zoo-Keep would just up and leave and have the volunteers work unsupervised?"

"So you mean…" Chloe trailed off.

"It's possible that something happened, something bad," Ember said. "What if he was taken as well?"

Chloe gasped dramatically. "You mean Nadie and now Professor Burke?"

Ember nodded. That was exactly what she was thinking. "Maybe they ran into some kind of unexpected trouble and are stuck there."

Chloe wrapped her arms around herself. "What are you getting at?"

What if Mallorus had shown up at the last place anybody would expect him to be? That way he could easily avoid detection. Ember shook her head. She was letting her imagination run wild. She had to stick to facts. Besides, Ember had to grudgingly admit that she would be no match against the dark sorcerer.

Ember's gaze inadvertently fell to the thick forest behind them, and a shudder passed through her. "We need to figure out what's going on.

But how?" Ember felt like she had come to a standstill with no further leads.

"I think the library might give us some answers," Chloe said. "Whenever I'm sad or confused, books always come to my rescue, and what better place to find answers than one place that has likely a million of them?"

"Sounds like a good idea," Ember said, even though she shuddered to even enter the library.

"Let's go," Chloe said, more excited than ever.

Chapter Fourteen

WILD GOOSE CHASE

The two girls stood at the threshold of the giant library, which was even grander than the amphitheater. There were shelves after shelves of books stacked as high as the ceiling. Ember couldn't help but gape at the dome-shaped structure.

Just as they entered, Summer walked towards them. She wasn't alone.

"Xander," Ember stammered. Xander was Summer's classmate and best friend at Zanith, and Ember's lifelong crush.

"Hey, kiddo," Xander said, ruffling Ember's hair. Unfortunately, he saw her as nothing more than a little kid. "What are you doing here?"

"Haven't you heard?" the blond girl next to him said. "She didn't make the cut to be a witchling. Poor little Amy is a remnant."

"It's actually Ember," she replied, shrugging Xander off and stepping away. She didn't like the other girl. She reminded Ember of an older version of Clarisse. In fact, she wouldn't be half-surprised if the two girls were siblings.

"Whatever," the girl said.

Summer was frowning at her friend, but she didn't say anything to dissuade her, which made Ember angrier. Maybe she even agreed with her views.

"Come on, let's go," Summer said.

"Doesn't it bother you, Summer, that your sister is, well, a remnant?" the girl said, looking all haughty.

"Can we not do this now, Talis?" Xander said. He looked tired.

"Fine," Talis said, flipping her hair behind her back and walking up the spiraling staircase that disappeared somewhere on the upper levels. "I don't want to be in this stupid place anyway. Didn't they have anywhere else to send us? Glofiara is the last place that Mallorus would want to attack, considering the fact there are no real witches around."

Ember was seething at her words, and worse, her sister had said nothing to protest it.

"Let it go, Ember," Chloe said.

Ember wasn't ready to go. In fact, she was ready to give Talis a piece of her mind. She started to walk to the stairs but was interrupted by a loud cough. It was Mother Irene.

"What do you think you're doing?"

Ember bit her lip. She had forgotten that Mother Irene was the librarian. "I just wanted to go upstairs to check out the books."

Mother Irene narrowed her eyes before pointing to the wall on the opposite side. A list of rules were printed on it, the first being: no remnants allowed past the first level.

"That seems unfair," Ember said.

"Rules are rules," Mother Irene said. "You'll find whatever you need right here. The upper levels are for warlocks or other advanced-level magical community members. There's nothing for your use there."

"Fine," Ember said, grumbling and walking away.

Mother Irene cleared her throat once again. "Please see rule number three."

"No shoes allowed in the library," Chloe read out.

"Exactly," Mother Irene said. "This place is as sacred as the temple. Take your shoes off and make sure you don't make any noise or I'll be forced to write you up."

Ember rolled her eyes as she walked away. "I think she made that rule herself."

Chloe giggled under her breath. "I wouldn't put it past her."

Ember smirked before looking up at the daunting pile of books. "So where exactly do we begin?"

"I think we need to learn all about the forest to prepare us for what we might encounter in its depths."

"Good idea," Ember said. She walked to each shelf and started to pull down anything that remotely mentioned the forest or Glofiara. By the time she had finished browsing, she had more than thirty books that she promptly settled on the long table. A few students who were studying or doing their homework looked up at them, annoyed.

"That's too many books!" Chloe said, scraping a chair out and sitting down. "But I guess we have to start somewhere."

"Sure," Ember said, flipping the first leatherbound book open. It was so old that it made her sneeze right away, one into the other. By the time she was done, her throat was aching. "Ugh, these books are so old."

"Some older than our parents too," Chloe said, coming back to the table with a fresh stack. "Look what I found." She held up a book.

"An almanac?" Ember guessed.

"No, silly," Chloe said. "It's an old photo album of every fledgling class of Glofiara taken in the last twenty years."

"Why do we need it?" Ember asked curiously, thinking about the group photo they had taken the first day at Glofiara. She was pretty sure she was scowling at the photographer. Ember never took good pictures.

"Not for our mission," Chloe said. "But a few of my foster siblings studied here before I did. I was just curious."

"Sure," Ember said, immersing herself in the book, but she couldn't concentrate. Her mind inadvertently kept wandering to the forbidden upper section that only warlocks like her sister and her stuck-up friends were privy to. It was rather unfair.

Suddenly, next to her, Chloe gasped.

"What is it?" Ember asked, checking to see if a rat had run under the table.

Chloe moved the book she was reading towards Ember so she could see as well. She pointed at a picture on the upper-right hand section—class of 2002. It was taken over twenty years ago, but the person in the picture was unmistakable.

"Nadie?" Ember asked.

Chloe nodded. "I thought so."

Ember traced her finger over the glossy paper. The girl in the picture had the same unruly, curly hair Nadie had, only she had yet to learn how to tame it, and the same dark brown eyes.

"It must be some mistake. Nadie's not a remnant, she's a warlock," Ember said. Her head was still reeling from what she had found.

"Yeah, maybe it's someone else," Chloe said. "Maybe she has a twin or something?"

"Right," Ember said. But Nadie hadn't mentioned a sister. Now that she thought about it, Nadie hadn't even mentioned if she had a living family. The two girls stared at the picture for a few beats before putting it away. But Ember couldn't get the picture out of her mind. Was it possible that Nadie had been a remnant and had found a way to stabilize her power over time and graduate into a warlock? If so, she would have told her. Summer had also told her that it was next to impossible to make the transformation. But of late, her sister appeared more of a stranger.

"It could even be a cousin, or someone who looks really like her or maybe it's just the picture quality. I mean, it's kind of old and blurry," Ember reasoned.

Chloe nodded. "Yeah, you're probably right."

A large book thumped on the table next to her, making Ember look up. It was Elias. He nudged his chin at her book. "You're looking in the wrong place."

Ember scowled at him. "You don't even know what we're looking at."

"I just assumed that you're still on that wild goose chase."

Ember's cheeks colored. "It's not a wild goose chase."

"I think you're rather bored, or just too inspired by your parents," Elias countered.

He was dangerously close to the truth, but not quite. "I'm not bored," Ember said. "I'm concerned because nobody else is." Her voice rose with every word until Mother Irene glared at her, rapping her duster against one of the shelves a little too loudly.

Ember dropped her voice to a hiss. "Nadie is gone and nobody cares. They're all busy worrying about—"

"The worst sorcerer to ever exist?" Elias said. "Yeah, I'm sure he'll have some precedence over a schoolteacher."

"But what if the events are related?" Ember shot back.

"You mean he kidnapped Nadie?" Elias said with a sigh as if Ember were an impertinent child. "Are we still on that?"

"Stop doing that," Ember said.

"Fine," Elias said. To her surprise, he pulled out a chair and sat down next to her. "I shouldn't dismiss your concerns. You're worried about Nadie, I get it."

"And I have to do this for my sanity."

"I get that too," Elias said. He nodded at Nadie's logbook, which he still had in his arms. He had a second book next to it, thicker than any Ember and Chloe had pulled off the shelves. "I made your job easier for you."

He pointed to each of the botanical ingredients listed in the logbook. "Together these are used to treat a great injury—a burn of some kind or a searing of the flesh, most likely a magical wound."

Ember raised a brow. "Magical? But why would any magic user harm animals?" Use and practice of magic on animals had been banned twenty years ago.

Elias shrugged. "I don't know, but these plants thrive in cold temperatures, which means that—"

"They're found in the heart of the forest," Ember said. "Where no sunlight penetrates."

"You're smarter than I thought," Elias said. He pulled up a chair next to her. "Nobody goes into the southern trail, the part of the forest that sits right behind Glofiara. They say there's a terrible swamp there guarded by one of Mother Ethilenne's outcast brothers himself. Probably Timonus."

Ember snorted. "I don't believe in myths."

"Well, some of the more superstitious teachers do. In fact, we have a whole feast here at Glofiara during All Hallows' to please him."

A shiver ran down Ember's spine, despite herself.

"We'll see about that," Ember said, but she couldn't get Elias's words out of her head for the rest of the day.

Chapter Fifteen

THE WITNESS

They were at a dead end with no prospects. Ember kept staring at her to-do list. She had no idea what she was going to do next. Her time as an investigative agent seemed rather short-lived. It had been four days, yet there seemed to be no sign of Nadie. Ember had already made several trips to her office in hopes that she had returned, but it was always locked. Worse yet, she had been replaced in the Creativity class by a sub called Professor Wesley who couldn't care less about teaching them to stabilize their powers.

Ember watched the flame on her fingertip flicker and come to life. She had been practicing hard, but she couldn't summon a bigger one than that, and she didn't want to force things lest it grew out of control like the last time.

With Nadie gone, Chloe and the other non-magics were no longer welcome at the Creativity class; they were given the rest of the period off. But Chloe always waited for Ember outside the classroom. Ember felt a pang. Despite herself, she felt her heart melting. Besides, every great agent needed an assistant, right? She had seen the way her parents operated. They were partners—even before they got married. They complemented each other well, and Ember knew that it took both of them to solve a particular case. That was why they always went on assignments in pairs.

"I was thinking," Chloe said. "We could maybe conduct interviews."

"Interviews?" Ember asked. "Why?"

"I mean, we need to trace Nadie's last steps. Someone must have seen something we missed," Chloe said, biting her lip. "Or maybe that's just a really dumb idea. Just ignore me."

"Actually, no," Ember said, sitting up in bed. "That's a great idea. We need witnesses."

"Witnesses?" Chloe asked.

"I mean people who saw Nadie last," Ember explained hastily. "What's the plan?"

The next day was Friday, which meant classes were over at noon. Armed with Chloe's video-cam and Ember's gutsy attitude, the two girls set forward to interview. They began with their classmates first. The upperclassmen were scarier. They glared at them or downright shooed them away, but a few of them—the ones who liked Nadie—actually spoke to them. People had seen her at some point the day before she disappeared, but nobody could confirm where they saw her last.

"It'll take us hours to get through all of this footage," Chloe whined. "And nobody has a clear answer."

Even Ember was feeling demoralized. Nobody knew where Nadie went, and they couldn't talk to people too widely. They had already started asking questions, and the last thing Ember wanted was word of this to travel to the headmistress, or worse, her parents, who were still on campus.

Ember and Chloe were sitting on a stone bench in the inner courtyard waiting for the rain to stop. The peace was broken when Clarisse and her cronies walked up to them. Ember groaned internally and was about to leave when Clarisse blocked their way. She tossed her shiny blond hair at her back—the action reminding Ember so much of her sister. "I heard you guys were interviewing people."

"Not you," Ember said. "Besides, I thought you didn't like being recorded."

Clarisse's brows dropped. "Heard you were asking around about Nadie's whereabouts? What's wrong with her? Do you know something?"

Ember felt her stomach sinking. This was a bad idea. "No, not really. We were just concerned that she wasn't teaching classes and was replaced by someone else."

"Why are you so obsessed with her? It's really weird," one of Clarisse's cronies said. Parker was notably absent from the group today. "I mean, I'm pretty sure we got a better replacement."

Ember worked to get her fury under control. She didn't want to engage with Clarisse again and accidentally blurt out something she wasn't supposed to. "Chloe, let's go."

Chloe nodded. The girls started to walk away when Clarisse called out, "Pretty sure you want to talk to me. I was the one who saw her last, after all."

Ember whirled around to face her. "Excuse me?"

Clarisse stood with her hands on her hips. "That's right. I'm pretty sure I was the last person to see her. And guess what? She was headed into the Whispering Woods."

"Do you think she was messing with us?" Chloe asked.

"Obviously," Ember said. "Unless..." Clarisse was vapid and hated Ember's guts, and she had probably said it to mess with Ember's head. And it was working. It lined up with the theory that Ember already had about Nadie's disappearance. She couldn't simply shake it off. She kept thinking about it all the way to dinner, only half-noticing when Elias sat down at the table opposite them.

"I thought you didn't want to associate with us," Ember said.

Elias shrugged. "I mean, my options are pretty limited. So, what are you guys thinking? I heard you were interviewing people for a documentary on Nadie."

Ember raised a brow. "Is that what people are saying?"

"That's definitely what Clarisse is saying. She thinks you're in some kind of a cult dedicated to Nadie," Elias said. "It's harmless unless it catches a teacher's ears."

"Well, we're done with that," Chloe said. "It was a total bust."

"But it did give me some ideas," Ember said.

Elias leaned forward on the table. "What kind of ideas?"

Ember took a deep breath. It was the first time she was about to say her theory out loud. She felt almost stupid, but she needed to do it. "Travis Burke, the Zoo-Keep, he's missing too. What if he and Nadie went into the forest together and saw something they weren't supposed to?"

"Like Mallorus just chilling around in the forest?" Elias said.

Ember poked his arm. "Stop doing that. I never said anything about Mallorus."

"Fine, fine," Elias said. "So now you're saying two of our teachers have gone missing?"

"Looks that way," Ember said. "I just mean that they could have fallen into some kind of trouble in the forest. Professor Patel said it herself: the forest is unpredictable."

Suddenly the mystery was becoming clearer and clearer to her. She felt a twist of excitement in her gut and wondered if this was what her parents felt when they were on a hunt. Suddenly, the vision of her future became much clearer. She could keep being safe at school and learn to suppress her magic, or she could go out there and do something that was actually important.

Sure, the adults were out there doing the important job of finding Mallorus, but Ember could still make a difference here. She could bring Nadie home. She could show her sister that she wasn't just a dangerous freak.

"I need to check out the forest," Ember said.

"Excuse me?" Elias said. "Did you just hear what I said?"

"I hear you, and I heard what Headmistress Kinnera said, but I still need to find out."

Chloe looked at her wide-eyed. "I can't let you do that. Going in there is suicide. Elias, come on, say something."

Elias seemed to ponder something. Finally, he said, "If you do want to go into the forest, you have to do it at midnight. That's when the patrolling warlocks change their shifts."

"Thanks for the tip," Ember said while Chloe glanced between them in outrage. "Are you guys serious?"

"She's crazy," Elias said. "She's going in there whether you want it or not."

Ember looked up at him in surprise. Elias seemed to get her, and despite herself, she couldn't crack a smile.

"I agree it's suicide though, so if you are devoured by a flesh-eating tree or something, don't blame me," Elias said. "I'm not responsible."

"I won't," Ember said with a laugh.

"I might accompany you—but only until the edge of the forest. I want to see if you're actually stupid enough to do it," he continued. Just when Ember thought that Elias could actually be nice.

"There's no need for that," she said.

"I insist," Elias said.

"I'm with you, Ember," Chloe said stoically. "If Nadie is really in the forest, then we are going to bring her back."

"It's kind of stupid—and a lot crazy," Ember pointed out.

"I know," Chloe said. "But you're my friend."

Ember started to disagree but finally nodded. "Yes," she said. "You are my friend." Something between them had fundamentally changed, and Ember wasn't afraid of it anymore.

Chapter Sixteen

THE WHISPERING WOODS

At midnight, when Ember and Chloe were certain that everybody else had gone to sleep, they snuck out of bed. Everything was eerily quiet in the corridors outside, almost as if they were walking down the hallowed halls of a long-abandoned mausoleum. Each step they took seemed to echo down the halls. They followed the shadow and stuck to it as they managed to leave the school behind.

They were walking down the stairs when Chloe groaned. "Oh no."

Ember's heart lurched as her gaze darted around. Did someone find them? But there was nobody in sight.

"What is it?" Ember asked.

"My talisman broke," Chloe said in dismay.

"It's fine, we'll fix this later. Just put it away for now," Ember said. "Besides, there isn't any reason non-magics should be wearing it anyway."

"Right," Chloe said.

It was chillingly cold outside, but Ember didn't dare light the Glo-torch of her comm-device, in fear of being caught.

Elias told them that he would meet them at the South Trail, but Ember didn't believe him until she saw him standing at the very edge of the forest. "You came," he said, his teeth chattering against the cold.

"I'm surprised you did," Ember said.

"I was wondering if you truly have the Pearson courage," Elias said.

"Your obsession with my family really weirds me out," Ember said.

"I'm only an admirer," Elias said. "I've followed your parents' techniques closely; they're the greatest white sorcerers we have ever seen—the greatest pair ever made."

"Yeah, yeah," Ember said. This was something she had heard before.

"What are you guys sneaking around here for?" came a voice behind them. It was close enough to scare even Ember out of her wits, and for a quickening heartbeat, she felt her soul leave her body. Chloe screamed, and someone put a hand over her mouth to muffle the sound. It was Parker. "Shh," he said. "It's just me."

"What are you doing here?" Ember hissed.

"I followed this one out of the room," Parker said, nodding at Elias, who was scowling through the glaze of the moon above them. "He wasn't exactly inconspicuous."

"What do you want?" Ember asked warily. No doubt he was here to tattle on them.

"Must you always make me the villain?" Parker said sardonically.

"Actions speak louder than words," Elias muttered.

"You're going to get us caught," Ember hissed. "And maybe even expelled."

"Correction: you're the one looking for trouble," Parker said. "What are you doing out here anyway? Don't tell me you actually listened to what Clarisse had to say."

Ember looked up at him sharply. "How do you know about that?"

He shrugged. "Clarisse has been going around telling everybody how she made a fool out of you. Even I didn't think you would be that gullible."

"Wait, is that why you're here?" Chloe said. "Did you come to check up on us?"

"Like I said, I followed Elias out. I don't actually care what you do," Parker said, his arms folded over his chest. "Not like we are friends or anything, but it's your grave."

"None of us are actually allowed to be here," Chloe pointed out. "And you are supposed to be in detention for your prank on Elias."

From the look on Parker's face, it was clear that he was finally realizing that.

"Why are you here?" Parker insisted.

"Just following up on a hunch. With Nadie gone and now Professor Travis, as well."

Parker blinked. "Wait, you think somebody kidnapped them both? Are you listening to yourself?"

"If you have nothing better to add—" Elias began.

"You idiots, Professor Burke didn't go anywhere. In fact, he came back just this evening. I spoke to him. So whatever theory you've been cooking up, well, it's a load of toad dung."

Ember blinked. "So you mean that—" Before she could finish her sentence, voices drew closer to them, and the sound was strangely familiar.

"Hide," Ember said.

"Where?" Elias said, looking bewildered. "There's nothing but an open field."

Instinctively, the four of them turned to face the forest looming over them. "No way," Elias said, taking a step back. "No way I'm going in there."

Parker took him by his shoulder and shoved him into the darkness. "We don't have any choice, pretty boy."

Chloe walked right behind them. Ember followed them but stopped and peered behind once. It was her father...there was no doubt about it. He had his familiar blue Glo-torch in his hand, and he was talking to a hooded figure in the dark. Before Ember could decipher who the cloaked figure was, she felt a strange tug towards the forest.

"We have to go," Parker was saying. "They might see us."

He was right. But the only way to hide was inside the forest. With a deep breath, Ember followed the rest of them in.

She banged on the end of the Glo-torch, and it slowly flickered to life.

"Who do you think it was?" Parker asked.

"Probably a patrolling warlock," Elias said.

Both of them were wrong, but something made her keep that information to herself.

A chill crept up her shoulder where they stood.

"How long do we have to stay here?" Parker said. "They're probably gone."

He made a move to exit the forest when there was the unmistakable sound of a twig breaking. Ember used her Glo-Torch to determine the source.

"What was that?" Elias said, shooting a glare at Parker. "Don't tell me it's one of your pranks."

Parker scowled. "What are you talking about? I didn't do anything."

Ember flashed her Glo-torch around, the arc of light illuminating the trees surrounding them. There was nothing.

"Probably just a false alarm," she said.

"The forest is making me jittery, like the time I snuck coffee from my foster mom's mug," Chloe said.

"I still think he was behind it," Elias said, nodding at Parker. "What is he doing here anyway? It's probably one of his nefarious plots to scare us."

"Seriously? Who says nefarious?" Parker rolled his eyes. "Besides, my life doesn't revolve around you. Can we all agree that we hate each other and move on?"

"I don't hate you," came Chloe's small voice.

"I wasn't very nice to you in the beginning," Parker reminded her. Maybe it was just Ember's imagination, but she thought she heard the twinge of guilt in his voice.

Around them, there was a low hiss, and a single phrase drifted through the air, repeated multiple times. *Get out, intruders,* the voice whispered.

Elias scowled. "Is that one of your friends? Because if this is a joke, it's not very funny."

Parker frowned. Around them, the whispers increased to a loud hiss. "I have no idea what you're talking about."

The hair at the back of Ember's neck stood up. Parker was telling the truth, because the sound was positively inhuman. "It's the forest," Ember yelled. "Run."

The children broke into a sprint. Ember didn't know where she was going; she just ran blindly. The four children screeched to a halt at the clearing.

"If this is—" Elias began, but the rest of his words were cut off when a fibrous root entangled itself around his feet and swung him off the ground.

"Elias," Ember screamed, but he had vanished into thin air. She looked around, and even Parker and Chloe were gone. Ember ran blindly. She didn't know where she was racing, and at some point, she had lost her Glo-torch.

Ember was lost in the woods and had no idea how she was going to get out.

Chapter Seventeen

THE GATEKEEPER

Ember didn't know where she was, but her gut told her that she was even deeper in the forest than she had been before. Headmistress Kinnera wasn't lying when she said that the forest hated the remnants.

Ember looked around as her vision adjusted to the darkness. All magic users, remnants or otherwise, had superior vision to human beings, so it wasn't hard for her to get used to the darkness. It was eerie, because she had never used this particular ability before.

There was rustling in the bushes a few feet away. Ember jumped to her feet just as a figure leaped out. She scrambled to find a stick and raised it above her just as—"For Ethilenne's sake, it's me," Parker said, his body taut, his arms raised to block her attack.

Ember put the stick down. "Parker?"

"Last time I checked." He rubbed the back of his head. "Where's Chloe and my annoying roommate?" Parker said.

Ember shook her head. "They aren't here." Dread squeezed her chest as she processed what had happened. "The forest attacked us."

Parker made a face. "Yeah, now we're stating the obvious, because why not."

Ember rubbed her head. "Oh no."

"What did you think was going to happen when you ventured in here? This place is literally called the Whispering Woods. Creepy much?"

"Nobody asked your opinion," Ember snapped. She started to walk, but she didn't quite know where. "We need to find Chloe, and as much as I think Elias is snooty and all, we need to look for him too."

"Can't we just leave him here?" Parker said. "I'm sure he'll end up finding people he can annoy."

"Just stop," Ember said. "Let me concentrate."

"I think you'll need some help," Parker said. Smirking, he reached into his pocket and took out a compass. "We can use this to track our direction."

"Do you know which way Glofiara is?" Ember asked warily.

"I'm sure I'll figure it out," Parker said confidently.

Ember started walking. She couldn't wait for Parker, but he caught up to her. "Do you know where you're going?"

"No, but something is better than nothing," Ember said.

Parker glanced at her sideways. "You know your hero complex is what got us in trouble in the first place."

"Excuse me?" Ember blanched.

"Yeah," Parker said. "I mean, I get it. Growing up in your parents' shadow must be hard, especially seeing who they are. But you need to draw the line somewhere."

"You don't know the first thing about me," Ember said furiously. "And I didn't even want you here in the first place. You just showed up." Ember cupped her hands around her mouth and shouted, "Chloe? Elias, can you hear me?"

"Keep your voice down," Parker hissed. "We don't want to alert the forest of our presence. Maybe it thinks we're dead or something."

"How? We're literally moving around," Ember pointed out. She couldn't get his comment out of her head.

"Who cares?" Parker said. "We are safe...for now. We don't need to call more attention to ourselves. So just be quiet."

A horrible feeling came over Ember. "Do you think that Chloe and Elias..." The two stared grimly at each other.

"It's bad enough that we are practically ostracized from the magic community, and now we have a sentient tree after us. The world truly doesn't give us remnants any breaks."

"Maybe the forest doesn't realize we are remnants yet," Ember said.

"What do you mean?" Parker asked.

"Think about it—our magic surges only when we use it, but what if we don't while we're in here? That way the forest can't differentiate us from a full-fledged magic user."

"It's possible," Parker admitted begrudgingly. "But remember what Professor Patel told us. It's treacherous to both remnants and full-fledged magic users."

Ember frowned. Something about Parker's words nudged at the back of her head. "You're right, but doesn't it seem odd, though?"

"What?"

"Why is it especially violent to us? There's no specific reason for it."

Parker stared at her. "Are you really bothering with the semantics of how or why the forest wants to kill us? We can think about that later when we're out of here," Parker said.

"We need to trace our path back. Maybe Elias and Chloe have already left."

"How do you intend to do that?" Parker asked.

Ember was about to answer his question when her gaze fell upon a tree trunk. She stopped to examine it more closely. It looked like a symbol of some sort—a half-moon sitting atop a circle. "What is this?" she murmured. A deep part of her memory nudged, slowly coming awake. "I've seen this somewhere before, but I can't remember where."

"I almost wish Elias were here," Parker said. "He would have known about all of this stuff." All of a sudden, he stiffened.

"Parker?" Ember said, reaching for him. Something felt very wrong about it, and the hair at the back of her neck stood up.

"Do you hear it?" Parker asked.

"Hear what?" Ember asked with a frown.

Parker began to walk away from her.

"Hey, where are you going?" Ember said, struggling to reach him, but he was too fast. "Parker, wait up."

To her horror, Parker walked up to an embankment that seemed to have appeared out of nowhere, surrounded by thick trees and hedges. Without hesitating, he walked into it, still in that trance-like state.

That was when Ember heard it too—that lilting voice. "You seek power," it said, so quiet that Ember felt the words dance across her bare skin. "You want to be as powerful as the rest of your family. They see you as weak and pathetic; they think nothing of you." Flashes of memories danced in front of her eyes—her parents hugging and loving her sister while she was cast aside, her parents being proud of Summer while they watched her with distrust. Her parents and her sister being the picture-perfect family while she was nothing more than an extra limb nobody wanted or asked for.

And then a particular memory sharpened to the point where Ember thought she was reliving it again. It was fourth grade; the Pearsons had been living in Ireland, and Ember was participating in soccer—a human game. Her parents had insisted that they would come. But when the game kicked off, there was no sign of her parents. Later on, they apologized for not making it. They had found a new lead and they had to check up on it as soon as possible. There was always a bigger priority. Ember never played soccer again.

Tears formed in Ember's eyes. She nodded as the whispers increased in volume in her head, almost like a thousand voices were speaking at once. "You seek power. Come close; I'll give you what you want."

A vision opened up in front of Ember. It was Zanith. Ember had only seen pictures of it on the postcards that her sister had sent home. It was always out of her reach. Until now...

She began to walk into the pond after Parker as the words swirled around her. As soon as the water rushed up her hip, her body realized something was wrong. Fire and water didn't mix, after all.

Ember snapped out of her trance, but it was already too late. Parker was just a few paces away from her. One minute he was there, and the next moment he vanished inside the inky depth of the water.

"Parker," Ember screamed. The sound caught in her throat as something strong grabbed her by her feet and dragged her under. She struggled for several minutes, the muddled water clouding her vision until she didn't know where the bottom was, or the top.

Her vision blackened as she was suspended in the water for several minutes, or maybe it was just a few seconds before something, or someone pulled her out.

Ember gasped as she landed on the shore and threw up the water stuck in her chest, coughing violently for several seconds. Parker was on his knees next to her.

"Did you...?"

Ember shook her head. She wasn't the one who had helped him out. But then who had? Beads of water rolled down his hair and face. Just like him, Ember was soaked. They helped each other off the wet floor and looked around. "Where are we?"

They were standing in a clearing in front of a massive stone gate. Sconces were placed on tall iron pillars leading up to it, casting a garish light on the harsh features of the landscape.

"Are we..." Parker trailed off.

Ember shook her head. "Don't say it."

"We're dead, aren't we?" Parker said. "The forest got to us at the end."

"You have to stop saying that," Ember said, striding forward.

"Where do you think you're going?" Parker said.

"Maybe you don't want to get out of...whatever this place is, but I do," Ember said.

Parker pointed his chin at the vast pond behind them. "Do you see that? That's the gateway for the dead."

"Quiet," Ember said. "Let me think."

"Saint Apostha. Saint Gleeona. Mother Ethilenne, save us from our Undoing, welcome us into your fold," Parker murmured under his breath as he said his final prayers.

"You have to stop saying that," Ember said. "We're okay. We're not dying." Ember didn't know if she was pacifying herself. She took off her talisman and flicked her finger. Immediately, an ember of fire came alive on her fingertips that sent relief crashing into her. "Look, I can still use my powers. We are not dead. This isn't the afterlife."

"Well it still looks like it," Parker murmured. "Look at the sky, it looks like it was made from flecks of fire and ice."

Ember had noticed. "There must be some way out."

As if on cue, there was a strange rumbling around them as stone carvings shot out of the ground, narrowly hitting Ember, who jumped out of their way. The large stone door opened with a loud groan that grated her skin. A figure was seated on some kind of altar, his arms on either side of the chair.

"Trespassers," he hissed, his voice echoing around them. And then he sniffed, as if trying to smell them. "Remnants."

"So you just smelled us, huh? Not creepy at all," Parker said.

"Stop that," Ember said.

"Silence," said the figure, standing up from his chair. He had long, flowing, silver-white hair, wore dark clothes like a priest, and most importantly…

"You're blind," Ember observed. "You can't see us."

He leaned on a staff. "You're trespassing on my lands as you've done before, and I don't deal kindly with trespassers."

"We have never been here before."

The dark figure sniffed the air. "You do not lie."

"Of course we don't," Ember said, looking around at the rolling knolls of wasted land. Who would want to be here by their own choice? "We are not the trespassers you seek."

"And what do *you* seek?" the figure bellowed, making Ember cringe.

"Who are you?" Parker asked. "And what is this place?"

"There's a price to pay for your answer. First, tell me what you seek here," the figure said.

"We're here by mistake; we were looking for our friends," Ember said, stepping forward.

The figure seemed to consider their words before he finally said, "I'm the Gatekeeper, and you're in the Triad of Dreams, my kingdom."

Ember and Parker exchanged a glance. Ember wasn't superstitious, but she knew exactly who the Gatekeeper was—Ethilenne's forgotten brother, Timonus. She had heard the myths. Timonus was real. Did that mean Ethilenne was real too?

Elias had warned her about this, but she had dismissed it, thinking it was a myth out of a fairytale. How could she believe it when she had believed in science over superstition, facts over stories, all her life?

"You're real," Parker said in awe.

"Of course I am, silly mortal," the Gatekeeper said.

"You stole Ethilenne's powers; you wanted it all for yourself and that's why she banished you," Ember said, trying to remember what Chloe had told her about the two brothers of Ethilenne.

The figure lurched forward, slamming the staff on the ground thrice. "You're mistaking me for my other brother. I was framed."

Parker and Ember exchanged another look.

"Why do you seek me, human?" the self-professed Gatekeeper said.

"We have lost our way," Parker said.

"Lies," the Gatekeeper said. "You came here seeking something you desperately want."

"Please, our friends are in danger and—"

"You cannot stand each other," he interrupted again. Ember's temper flared. He wasn't the good guy, and he definitely wasn't going to cooperate. "I was punished for my brother's crimes, abandoned here to guard time, never to get old. In a way, I'm no better than a prisoner. I can tell a lie from a truth, facts from a story. You found your way because of your greed, because of an impossible thing you seek."

Ember swallowed hard. Was her dream of going to Zanith impossible, then?

"You don't know us," Parker said.

"But I do, mortal," the Gatekeeper said. "I have the answers to all your questions."

An idea struck Ember. She might not know much about the Ancient Ones, but she knew they were arrogant. "One of our teachers at the school has gone missing. Do you know where she is?"

Even though the Gatekeeper was blind, he looked straight at Ember. "You seek this woman…Willow."

"Nadie," Ember corrected.

"Quiet, human," the Gatekeeper said. "You are in *my* realm."

"So you keep saying."

"You have a rather sharp tongue, child."

"I don't mean to disrespect," Ember said, keeping her eyes down. The Ancient One seemed to consider her for a few moments. "An answer for an answer," he finally replied. A spark of hope dug in

Ember's heart. He could tell her where Nadie was. But why had he called her Willow? "But going down the path won't bode well for you."

"We're ready for anything," Ember said, taking a step forward.

"Are you kidding me?" said Parker, grabbing her by the arm. "You might have very well signed your life away to him."

"It gets lonely here," the Gatekeeper said. "Your thoughts can keep you company only for so long."

"He's totally nuts," Parker said under his breath, glancing at the Gatekeeper.

"Yeah, he's been stuck here for a long time," Ember said, looking around. She felt the air stifling her already, and she had been here for less than an hour. How must he feel? Thick smoke emanated in the distance, wrapping itself into the ground. Time seemed to stay still here, the seconds stretching into eons that never really moved forward. Tiny flecks appeared in her vision as she looked around at the thousands of brilliantly burning orbs that floated midair. Were they the unfortunate souls that the Gatekeeper had managed to trap?

"Banished—he tried to steal from Ethilenne, remember?" said Parker.

"Lies," the Gatekeeper said, his booming voice making the two almost jump out of their bones.

"We have to find another way," said Parker.

Ember shook her head. "We have to listen to what he says. Otherwise, we have no way out."

"Very well," the Gatekeeper said. "What begins but never ends, the one thing precious to you more than anything else in the world? Once it gets taken away, it can never be returned."

"It's a puzzle," remarked Ember.

"Yeah, no brainer," Parker said.

"Give me the answer and you shall be rewarded in return," the Gatekeeper said.

"He's messing with us," Parker said.

"He's an exiled Ancient One," Ember hissed back. "What else do you expect? Now think what he might be trying to tell us through the puzzle."

"It's definitely not straightforward," Parker said, glancing at the Gatekeeper. "I don't trust him."

"It gets so terribly lonely, so lonely," the man muttered under his breath. The pillars around them shifted, rumbling as if they were human.

"Look," Parker said, pointing at small globes of light that had popped out around them. Each had a different color—some were bright red while others were striking blue.

Curiosity got the better of Ember, and she couldn't help stepping forward to examine a spinning globe. She placed a finger over it—apprehensive at first. The spinning globe was more translucent than anything else.

"Each one has a story to tell," said the Gatekeeper, as if right at Ember's ears. Before she knew what was happening, the globe in front of her grew larger in size. Inside, memories flashed by fast as a hurtling train. She saw images of a boy.

The boy was barely five, standing in front of a burning house while he heard distant screams.

"We must go," a voice said, putting a hand on his shoulder. "You will achieve great things one day. You're destined for it. You are the chosen one." The scenery changed, replaced by another. This time the boy was older. He was walking down a familiar street when he was pushed to the ground by a much older boy. "Freak," they screamed. "You're a freak."

The scene changed again—the boy was older, with shoulder-length, pale white hair. He was handsome and standing at the gate of Zanith. He was finally home.

A tall man walked towards him. "Welcome to your future."

"Ember," Parker called distantly. "Ember."

Ember shook her head, returning to reality. "Y-yeah?"

"What happened to you?" Parker asked. "I thought you spaced out for a few seconds."

"I think I saw somebody's memory," Ember said, shaking her head. "It was a little boy, but then he grew up and…"

"We don't have time to be distracted," Parker said. "We need to get out of here. I don't feel so good."

Ember felt the same way. It almost seemed like her body was turning to mush, as if she was made of jelly.

There were thousands and thousands of such spinning globes wherever Ember looked. "Memory," she thought. "He keeps them for himself."

"Something is wrong," Ember said. She turned her eyes upward, and what she saw made her gasp. Elias and Chloe were suspended inside twin globes of impenetrable, translucent spheres just like the memory balls.

"It does get so terribly lonely," the Gatekeeper said, and Ember finally realized what he was saying.

"Price to pay," she repeated under her breath. "He intends to keep us for himself."

"I told you not to make a deal with a freaking Ancient One," said Parker urgently. "We need to get out of here."

"Don't you get it?" Ember said, looking around. "We are trapped in here. Only *he* can get us out."

"Then we are doomed," Parker said. "I bet it's not a real puzzle at all. He intends us to fail."

Ember looked around desperately. "What if Nadie is trapped here as well?" she said.

"There are only six spheres," observed Parker. "The rest are all memories."

"She must be here," Ember insisted.

Parker grabbed Ember by the arm. "Why did he call her Willow?"

"He must be mistaken," said Ember.

Parker raised a brow. "An Ancient One is mistaken?"

"He's blind," Ember pointed out. "He might be able to make mistakes."

Parker looked down at his hands, which were slowly being rendered to a jelly-like state. "Oh my Ethilenne, what's happening to me? Think fast, Ember."

"I-I can't," Ember said in a panic as she ran the puzzle through her head. The most precious thing in the world. What did it mean? It differed for different people.

"What's the thing you want most in the world?" Ember asked.

"To be a good son and take care of my mom," Parker said without any hesitation.

Ember was almost ashamed to admit that there was something she wanted more than that—to prove herself.

"That's not it," Ember said. "It's alluding to something else." She closed her eyes as the words of the puzzle swam in front of her.

"We're going to be trapped," Parker said. "We're running out of time."

Ember's eyes snapped open. That was it; that was what the Gatekeeper meant. He was alone, obsessed with his own image.

"Time," she said. "Time is the most precious thing in the world. If you put us in a prison, you take our freedom away, but with that so does time. You can never get your time back."

The Gatekeeper seemed to consider her words. Ember held in a breath, waiting for the Gatekeeper's answer.

"Very well," he said. "You're right. Now, ask for what you want in return in a single breath."

"Return my friends and me to the human realm without harm, and tell me a woman called Nadie's fate."

"You can choose only one," the Gatekeeper warned. "I already told you. Don't be greedy, girl."

Ember closed her eyes. She remembered Nadie's face, and how she was the only person who truly believed in Ember. Tears streamed down her face as she said, "Return me and my friends Parker, Chloe, and Elias safely back to the human realm." She was so close to finding out where Nadie was, but saving Chloe and Elias was more important.

"Very well," the Gatekeeper said. There was disappointment laced in his voice, almost as if he wanted something different. "Do not return here again, and be careful of the time that approaches. It is grim indeed."

There was a bright flash of light before everything went dark. Ember woke up with her cheeks pressed to the cold, hard floor of the forest. She spat out the bitter earth in her mouth and sat up.

The others were slowly waking as well—all three of them. Elias' glasses were cracked, and there was dirt all over his body; the rest of them looked no different.

"We did it," Parker said, laughing hysterically. "We escaped."

Ember turned her chin up when she felt the warmth of the sun on her skin. It was daylight. She looked down at her hands. No more jelly.

Chloe groaned, rubbing her head. "What happened?"

"Basically, you guys were kidnapped by an Ancient One, and me and Ember saved you."

Elias frowned. "You're making that up."

"I remember wading into the pond," Chloe said. "Somebody was calling my name. They told me that they would show me who my real parents are."

"The voice said my father would come back to me," Parker said. "I knew it was impossible. He has been dead for many years."

Only Elias kept quiet.

Ember cleared her throat. "It said that it would grant me stable powers, just as I have always wanted."

The four children were silent.

"What happened then?" Elias finally asked. Parker gave them both a short rundown. According to Parker and Ember, they had been knocked out cold the moment they sank into the water.

"But something saved me," Ember said. "It pulled me out of the water conscious."

"Me too," Parker said. "It's the only reason we are alive."

"So you solved the puzzle of an Ancient One to get us out unhurt," Elias said, shaking his head. "And I wasn't awake to see any of that?"

"You've got that right," Parker said, smirking. "I guess you owe me one now."

Ember expected Elias to retort, but instead he surprised her by saying, "Thanks. You saved our lives."

Parker exchanged a glance with Ember, and she could tell that he hadn't been expecting that either.

"So, are we, like, friends now?" Chloe said, beaming at everyone.

"Now you're taking it a step too far," Elias said, but he was smiling.

Even Ember smiled. "I was never the superstitious one," she said with a shrug.

"But this means Ethilenne and all the rest of the stories are true," Chloe said with awe. She kissed the back of her hand before touching it to her forehead. "Ethilenne bless us all."

"Ethilenne or not, I'm glad we're safe," Elias said, turning to Parker and Ember. "So thank you."

"Thank you, gai," Chloe said to Parker. "Gai" was an honorific for older brother. "I mean, is it okay if I call you that?"

"Only if I get to do this," Parker said, ruffling Chloe's hair good-naturedly.

Before any of them could say anything, they heard the unmistakable sound of footsteps growing closer. Summer came into the clearing, stopping dead when she saw the four of them caked in mud.

"We can explain," Ember said, thinking of the punishment that would be awaiting them when Headmistress Kinnera found out. And she knew that Summer wouldn't hesitate for a second to turn her in.

Instead, Summer walked up to Ember and said, "We need to talk."

Ember could sense something was wrong. Summer looked disturbed, and she hadn't asked a single question about their whereabouts or berated her on sight. "What is it?"

Summer took a deep breath. "They're saying Mom and Dad helped Mallorus escape."

Chapter Eighteen

THE ZOOKEEPER

Ember came to her feet. "They're saying what now?"

Summer nodded somberly. "Yeah, the Conservation Society launched an investigation, and they found clues that led them to believe that Mom and Dad are responsible."

"That's a load of—" Ember stopped herself before she said a bad word. "That's impossible. You know it."

"I do," Summer said, nodding. "But they have no way to prove their innocence."

"What kind of clue did they find?" Elias asked.

"I'm not sure. The Society is being rather tight-lipped about it, and even us apprentices aren't supposed to know anything. They're taking them away to be investigated while you are—" Summer sent her a scathing look. "What are you doing here exactly?"

The four of them looked at each other. They had to straighten out their story before they got into trouble. "Actually—" Chloe began, but Parker put his hand over her mouth to make her stop.

"Yes?" Summer asked. "None of you showed up to your morning classes. Your absence was noticed."

Ember sighed in relief. At least no one had noticed that they had been missing since last night.

"We were out on a morning stroll," Elias said.

"All four of you?" Summer asked. It was obvious that she didn't believe their story one bit.

"Yep," Parker said, giving her a sunny smile. "We got into a small disagreement and accidentally ended up here."

"Inside the forest?" Summer echoed.

"We were only here for five minutes before you found us," Ember said. "We tripped and almost fell in a swamp. Be careful, it's right there."

Summer jumped at her words. Ember snorted while her older sister made a face. "Very funny. Now come on, let's get you out before any of them notice you gone."

The four nodded somberly before following Summer. The Gatekeeper had deposited them right at the mouth of the forest. Just as they were walking up the front steps, they ran into Xander and Talis. Talis shot them a scowl. "Where have you been? We were running around looking for you."

Xander put a hand on Ember's shoulder, not caring that she was so dirty. She wished to disappear into the Earth. "Are you okay, kiddo?"

"Y-yeah, I'm fine," Ember said.

Talis glared at them. "We spent about an hour looking for you when we had better things to do. Where were you, anyway?"

Ember expected Summer to give her away and bit her tongue. To her surprise, Summer said, "They tried ditching their classes to hang out at the Menagerie. But the Zoo-Keep found them and alerted me of their presence."

Ember's eyes lit up. The Zoo-Keep was back. She had some questions that he needed to answer for her.

"I see," Talis said, but she didn't look like she believed them.

"Come, let's go," Summer said, turning to Ember. "Clean up and come down to meet Mom and Dad before they leave."

"I thought they already left yesterday night after dinner?" Ember asked. Now that they were back in the present world, she distinctively remembered her dad talking to a dark, hooded figure at the edge of the forest. She had to leave before she could be discovered, but she couldn't help but wonder who the figure was. Could there be, perhaps, some truth to the allegations made against them?

She shook her head. It was absurd and insane. They were the ones who had defeated Mallorus the last time, and according to the stories that she heard from other people, it had been nearly impossible. Why would they knowingly get him out?

She nodded to Summer, who left after squeezing her shoulder.

"So what happens now?" Parker asked, looking somber.

"I need to talk to my parents and figure out what's going on," Ember said. "Hopefully we haven't attracted too much attention at school."

"I think it's too late for that," Elias said, checking his comm-device. "Look at this message. Headmistress Kinnera wants to see Ember in her office tomorrow."

"Shoot," Ember said. She hadn't received the message because, she belatedly remembered, she had left her comm-device somewhere in the realm of the Gatekeeper.

"What do we do now?" Parker asked.

"First of all, we need to get our story straight," Ember said. "Then we'll go from there."

"See you guys at dinner then," Elias said. The two boys walked away. Ember had a weird feeling as she saw them leave. Were they friends now? Or maybe it was just a trauma bond they shared. Something between them had fundamentally changed, and Ember didn't know quite what to make of it.

Her father, George Pearson, was pacing the length of his room when Ember knocked on the door and walked in. Rosetta Pearson, who was sitting on the bed, almost leaped up to hug her. "Oh, Ember, where have you been? We were worried sick about you."

"It's rather silly. My friends and I went out on a morning stroll and—" She realized that her father was looking at her in a strange way. Did he perhaps remember seeing her in the dark yesterday? That was impossible. She had been very careful about it.

Rosetta stepped back, and Ember realized that she was gaping. "You have friends?"

"Why is that so surprising?" Ember asked warily.

"It's just that you don't usually do friends," George said, walking up to them.

Ember shook her head. "Let's not talk about me. What's going on with you two? Summer told me that—" She couldn't get the rest of the words out.

George and Rosetta glanced at each other. "It's just a little misunderstanding at the Society. They investigated Thanatos and found magic that they think may have our Trace."

Ember had heard about Trace from her parents. It was much like a magical fingerprint, unique to every user.

"The Dogamar team found it and traced it to us in the system." The Dogamars were a breed of highly-trained canines who assisted the sorcerers and warlocks during magical investigations.

"It has to be a mistake," George said. "Although I can't help but wonder..."

"Wonder what?" Ember asked.

George shook his head. "Don't concern yourself with our fate."

"How can I not?" Ember cried out. "I know you like to forget it, but you have two daughters, not one, you know?"

Rosetta and George frowned. "What is that supposed to mean?"

Ember shook her head. "Nothing," she said.

Rosetta's face softened. "Ember, we love you and your sister equally. You know that, right? There's no difference between you two for us."

Ember nodded, but deep down, she knew it wasn't true. She turned to her father and said, "Why did you guys stay back at Glofiara? Weren't you supposed to leave yesterday?"

"We were, but some work came up," her father said. His vague answer made Ember narrow her eyes. She helped them downstairs with their luggage and said goodbye at the gate. She wished she could leave with them, and Summer seemed to have the same idea, because she looked like she was on the verge of tears.

"Don't let your precious friends see that," Ember said.

Instead of heading back to the school—there was no point anyway, as she had missed half the day—she headed towards the Menagerie.

She found the Zoo-Keep right outside. He was a tall, lanky man with thick hair that covered the top of his head and an equally thick beard. He was carrying what looked like a big bag of manure.

"Hi," she said, walking up to him.

Travis Burke was a man in his forties. He glanced at Ember warily as he put the heavy sack down on the floor. For such a thin man, he sure could lug around a lot of weight.

"What do you want, little one?" Even though his words were gruff, his tone wasn't.

"Do you have a minute? I need to ask you something," she said.

"Go on," he said.

Ember cleared her throat. "Well, it's about the injured animal at the Menagerie."

"Are you talking about the Tekkow?" he said.

Ember blinked. She had no idea what he meant, but it only confirmed what she needed to know. "So there was an injured animal here?"

"Of course there was," Burke said. "But he's long gone now."

"Where did he go?" Ember asked.

"He was too much for me to handle by myself. Damn thing nearly took my leg off." He nodded at his feet, referring to his limp.

"I'm sorry about that," she said.

Travis chuckled. "Ain't the first time this has happened."

"So do you like it, then?" she asked. "Working with animals?"

Travis showed her a gap-toothed grin. "Of course I do; they're my whole life."

"Did Professor Owsmann promise you help?"

The man blinked in shock. "How did you know?" he said. For one second, Ember thought she caught an edge in his voice, but then it was gone.

"Just a theory," she said.

"Matter of fact, she did, but she never showed up like she promised." He sounded bitter.

Ember inhaled sharply. Maybe something had happened before Nadie got to help the wounded beast. But what?

"Did she go into the forest?" Ember asked.

"I mean, yeah, she did tell me some of the herbs would be found in the forest, but she never followed up with me on that. I didn't have the resources to keep the Tekkow here, even though I desperately wanted to, so I had to move it. I had to release it back into the wild without help. It had grown quite violent by that point. I wish Nadie had told me that she was leaving the school for a while; maybe the outcome would have been different," Travis said.

"Right," Ember said. That lined up with what Headmistress Kinnera had said, but Ember still couldn't believe that Nadie would abandon an injured animal, unless something else more pressing had come up. But what?

"When did this happen?"

"Two weeks ago, on Sunday," the man replied.

Ember counted in her head. So it was a day after Mallorus got out. According to the log book, Nadie had been in the school for the next two days before she left. But nobody had seen her since Sunday.

The timeline was clear, but Nadie's whereabouts were not. Maybe Elias was right. Maybe she had just conjured up a mystery that wasn't even there…just a wild goose chase. But her gut told her there was more to it, and she couldn't just shove it away. It was an insistent voice at the back of her head. Was it all about the hero complex like Parker had accused her of? Ember hoped not. That would mean that she had put her friends' lives in danger for no reason.

"What does she mean to you anyway?" Travis asked, his brows coming together.

"She's my favorite teacher," Ember said. They had spent a little over a month together, but Nadie had understood her better than anybody else in her life.

The man nodded. "She must mean a lot to you if you came here looking for her. I'm certain that she's safe."

Ember nodded, but despite his reassurances, she couldn't stop looking for her. Nobody else was, and she couldn't let her down either. "Thank you for your time," she said.

The man nodded and picked up the heavy sack again. Ember felt bad to see him work despite his injured leg. She wanted to offer help, but the man looked proud enough not to accept it.

Just as she was thinking this, the sky above her opened up, and it began to pour. The Gatekeeper's words echoed in her head as she tipped her face up to the sky to feel the rain on her face. A darker time was coming, and Ember didn't know what it would bring with it.

Chapter Nineteen

TRACES AND SIGILS

Elias, Ember, and Chloe were already at the table talking amongst themselves when Parker slid in beside Chloe. "What's up, guys?"

The three openly gaped at him, and so did most of the first-years. When Ember had suggested that they talk over dinner, she hadn't really expected Parker to abandon his more popular friends and sit with them at the table.

A few gaped in surprise, and Clarisse was openly fuming. Ember couldn't help but smile, and she covered it by busying herself drinking soupy noodles.

"Let's straighten out our stories first," Parker said.

Ember nodded at something behind him. "You do realize that your friends are waiting for you to join them?"

"Yeah," Parker said.

"And are you not?" Chloe asked.

"Can we just concentrate on what's important here first?" Parker said, sounding almost irritated.

"Fine by me," Ember said, shrugging. "I already told my sister we were out on a morning walk. Let's just stick to that."

"Sounds good," Chloe said.

"That might work for you, but most people won't believe we're friends," Elias said. "The teachers might have noticed that by now, and the headmistress isn't exactly a fool."

"We didn't just escape an Ancient One to be bested by a cranky old woman," Ember said. "We'll deal with her."

"I hope for your sake we do," Elias said. "I mean, things aren't exactly going well for your family. Did you speak to your parents?"

Ember hesitated, and then nodded. "Yeah, I did." She explained what had happened. "Do you have any theories?"

"I don't know much about Traces, but I guess we can find answers in the library," Elias finally said.

"There's something even you don't know?" Parker said, one of his brows raised.

"Oh shut up," Elias said.

"Here, I'll give you something else you probably don't know about," Parker said, taking a napkin and drawing a half moon on top of a circle.

Elias gave him a look. "You're messing with me."

"I'm not," Parker said.

"Do you know what symbol that is?" Ember asked, leaning forward on the table.

"Of course I do," Elias said. "It's the sigil of Mallorus."

Right on cue, a loud crash of thunder echoed over them, making the table rattle.

"To be more accurate, it's the sigil of his followers, the Order of Shadows. They brand it over their hearts to show their solidarity to him and his cause."

Ember's eyes widened. "You're joking."

"Of course not," Elias said, frowning. "Why would I joke about something like this?"

"It makes sense for that psycho to have a cult enshrined to him," Parker said. "Totally normal to follow the dark overlord."

"We don't know who these people are or their motives," Elias said. "We must focus on what we do know."

Ember nodded. That was why the symbol had seemed so familiar to her. She had seen it in one of her parents' old notebooks. They kept a detailed account of their missions, but they always made sure that those books remained out of the reach of Ember and Summer. "I wish we had taken a picture of it on our comm-device."

"That would have definitely been more useful," Elias agreed.

"The sigil in the forest," Chloe said, her eyes widening. "Does this mean that his followers are rising again?"

"I don't get it. What would they want in Glofiara—" Parker stopped suddenly. "Unless."

"Unless what?" Elias asked.

"Does that mean *he* is here, too?" Parker asked.

A chill passed through Ember. She remembered what Summer had said about Mallorus seeking out his followers. Suddenly, she didn't want her theory to be correct anymore. Until that moment, Ember had been treating the case like an adventure instead of one with actual stakes—like her life and those of her friends.

Chloe shivered. "Do you think Nadie is in trouble because of him? I mean, Ember already—" she started.

Elias shook his head. "You're forgetting something. Mallorus was last spotted all the way out in Asia."

"So it's one of his followers then?" Ember said. That made more sense. "Maybe they're waiting for him to come to his powers and using the sigil to pledge their allegiance to him?"

"A sigil is usually meta-physically connected to the one who draws the first symbol," Elias said.

"I didn't understand a single thing you just said," Parker said.

"It means," Elias said in an irritated voice, "that the sigil was used to summon the master, and in this case, Mallorus."

The four of them fell quiet.

Parker broke the silence. "So there's someone at Glofiara who is one of Mallorus' disciples?" he said. "That's horrifying."

"It could be anyone," Elias said. "And that makes it difficult for us to trust anybody at school."

"We need to be very careful of the next move we make and act inconspicuously."

"Right," Chloe said. She seemed happy just to be part of the conversation.

"Unfortunately, we don't have much proof," Elias said.

"We still have to tell the headmistress," Ember said. "As much as I dislike her, we need to inform the authorities."

Elias raised a brow. "What made you change your mind?"

"Don't you remember what happened in the forest? We're way over our heads," Ember said.

"She's right. If Mallorus' followers are involved in Nadie's disappearance, the headmistress will know what to do," Chloe said.

"And how exactly do you intend to say it without blowing our cover?" Parker said.

Ember sighed. "I'll figure it out. We have to say *something*. We can't exactly take them on alone."

"True," Elias said. "No offense, but one of us can't stay invisible, one is an out-of-control Firestarter, and another doesn't have magic at all. As for me, it's better I don't try to help.

"You're a psychic, right?" Ember said. "I never asked. What exactly is your power?"

Elias winced. "Try multiple. I-I have visions when I touch something, but it doesn't always work."

"What do you mean?" Ember asked.

"He's a clairvoyant," Chloe said.

Elias smiled weakly. "Not much use though. My psychic-radar is broken."

"How?" Parker asked.

"Sometimes I see the past, sometimes I see the future. I cannot control it, and afterwards, all I'm left with is a splitting headache."

"Wait a minute," Chloe said. "You saw something out in the forest, didn't you? You touched one of the symbols and flinched."

Elias rubbed his temple. "I saw vague images—one of them was of Professor Owsmann."

Ember gasped. "Why didn't you say something?"

"Well, my powers are unreliable. I didn't know if it was the past or the future. Maybe Nadie was there at some point."

"Before she got into trouble," Ember said. She couldn't believe Elias had kept it from her.

"Trust me, I saved us the trouble," Elias said. "This is the curse of being a remnant. We can't do anything right. You saw what happened in the forest. We barely got out of there alive. If we were full-fledged magic users, things would have been so much easier, but we aren't."

The four children became solemn. They knew that Elias was telling the truth.

"So what does it mean?" Chloe asked, breaking the silence.

"Well, we know that Nadie probably went into the forest, didn't she?" Ember said. "What if she saw whoever was drawing the sigil and was spotted? Maybe that person took her to make sure she doesn't expose them."

"That makes sense," Parker said. The others nodded in agreement.

"Well, well, well, isn't this a chummy little group?" said a voice dripping with poison.

Parker eyed her warily. "What are you doing here, Clarisse?"

"Came to check up on you. You didn't show up during class today, and I heard from a little birdie that you were hanging out with these losers," she said.

"I think you accidentally looked into a mirror," Ember chimed in. Chloe giggled.

"Is it really that funny, non-magi?" Clarisse said, narrowing her eyes at Chloe.

"Leave her alone," Parker snapped, surprising all of them, Clarisse most of all.

"What?"

"I said," Parker said slowly, "leave her alone. You shouldn't pick on her."

Clarisse laughed, but there was no humor in it. "Get off your high-horse. In case you forgot, you were right there with us."

"And I regret every minute of that," Parker said, staring down at the table. He finally looked up—this time at Chloe—and said, "I'm sorry about what I did. I'm ashamed."

Clarisse shook her head. "I can't believe this. I can't believe that you're choosing them over me."

"That's not true, Clar," Parker said. "We are still friends. If you apologize to Chloe, then—"

"I'm not doing that," Clarisse said, venom in her eyes. Her gaze dropped to his missing hand. "I was wrong to give you a chance. You're weak and pathetic just like them." With that, she turned on her heels and left.

Parker kept staring at the floor while his face flushed red. Everyone in the dining hall was looking at them. Even Ember, who wasn't easily affected, was squirming in her seat.

Chloe walked up to Parker and, to their surprise, hugged him. "Thank you, gai."

Parker simply nodded and hugged Chloe back. Even Ember felt her heart melt. She turned to look at the next table and glared. "What are you staring at? Mind your own business." Her sharp tone had the desired effect, and soon everybody had moved on from the little scene.

Ember turned back to her table. "So, we're in agreement then. It's time to go face the headmistress and tell her what we know," she said grimly.

be gone for urgent work

Chapter Twenty

THE SPY

Headmistress Kinnera's office was as intimidating and ancient as she was, almost like she had fashioned it after herself. It was as large as at least two classrooms. Most of it was filled with odd little trinkets. Ember was examining a particularly owlish-looking one until it fluttered away, right out of the single-paned glass window.

"So where were we?" Kinnera said, fixing Ember with a stare over her strange little teacup. It was crooked, but somehow didn't spill any tea.

"Right, so we were on a morning stroll," Ember began. She was interrupted by Kinnera putting a hand up, the dramatic sleeves of her mantle swishing around her. "So you, Elias, Chloe, and Parker were out together. That seems rather odd to me."

"Why?"

"I've heard from your instructors that you do not get along with each other. Parker and Elias were in a fight just the other day." She fixed Ember with another stare, one which was impossible to look away from. Ember realized, belatedly, that she didn't know exactly what kind of powers the headmistress had except for her meta-physical displays. She could very well be a clairvoyant like Elias. Some of the gifted sorcerers managed to have more than one ability.

"You're wrong, ma'am. That's exactly where we were—out on the grounds where everybody could see us."

"Right," Kinnera said. She obviously didn't believe Ember.

Ember swallowed. Now this part was going to be really tricky. "We could have sworn we saw somebody disappear inside the forest."

Kinnera quirked a brow. "Who?"

"I believe it was one of Mallorus' followers," Ember said.

The headmistress stared at her for a few moments before she started to laugh—no, guffaw, the sound reverberating around the office. Ember shifted in her seat uncomfortably.

"Let me get this straight: you just happened to be out in the morning where you saw a member of the Order of Shadows."

"I know how it sounds, but—"

"Either you think that I'm a very foolish person, Miss Pearson, or you're cunning enough to think you can get one over on me. I'll assure you that neither is true," Kinnera said. "Now, tell me the truth."

"We saw that—"

"Don't feed me lies, Miss Pearson," Kinnera said. "I don't know what exactly you and your little 'friends' are up to, but if I find out, it won't bode well. Your parents are already being investigated at the Society. We don't want to create more trouble for them, now, do we?"

Ember shook her head. Guilt coursed through her.

"I'm glad that you see reason," Kinnera said with a nod.

"But Nadic is still missing," Ember couldn't resist saying.

Headmistress Kinnera sighed. "She isn't missing. She's gone off on some work." Out of nowhere, a parchment appeared and dropped on the desk in front of Ember. It had a familiar, looping handwriting.

I'll be gone for three weeks on some urgent work. x

"I received this two days after she left," Headmistress Kinnera said with a sickly-sweet smile. "So, you see, you have nothing to worry about at all. You may go now."

Ember was almost relieved when she left the office. Inside, she had almost suffocated under the weight of the lies she was carrying around. But worse, she was no closer to finding Nadie than she had been a week ago.

The other three were waiting for her when she came out. They crowded around her expectantly.

"So?" Chloe said. "What did she say?"

"She practically laughed me out of the room," said Ember. "And I think she suspects that we were up to something."

"Well, we did take a huge gamble," Elias pointed out, ever the practical one. That earned him a scowl from Parker and Ember and a pout from Chloe, who was too nice to ever frown at someone.

"Also, she showed me this note that was supposedly from Nadie," Ember said, shaking her head. "But it felt rather odd to me."

"So you think she was lying about it?" Elias said. "But why would she do that? It makes no sense."

"Maybe she made it up herself so that Nadie's disappearance wouldn't be investigated," Ember suggested.

"That's absurd," Elias said. "Wait, what exactly are you implying?"

"What if...what if Headmistress Kinnera is the spy that we are looking for?" Ember said. The more Ember thought about it, the more her suspicions about the headmistress took root. She was, after all, very blatant about her dislike for Ember's parents. She would also know about the mechanisms of the forest. Maybe she had orchestrated everything and decided to blame them for it.

"You mean she's the one who drew the sigil in the forest?" Parker said. "Really, the headmistress?"

Ember nodded. "Or maybe she knows who is responsible. Either way, she has the power to sweep everything under the rug."

Elias seemed deep in thought. "Logically, it would make sense."

Ember smiled. At least someone believed her. "Nadie aside, we must find whoever this spy is. If we do, maybe the Society can take them in to figure out where Mallorus is. And once they get him, my parents will be freed."

"It's still a long shot," Parker said.

Ember's face fell.

"But it's better than doing nothing at all," Elias said. "Especially if our theory is right and Nadie's disappearance is indeed connected to the Order of Shadows."

Chloe squeezed Ember's shoulders. "Don't worry, we'll get to the bottom of this."

Ember nodded, but deep down she couldn't help but wonder if she was missing a piece of the puzzle. Who was the hooded figure her father had been talking to?

"I would be honored to be of aid to the legendary George and Rosetta Pearson," Elias said. "They were my idols growing up."

"I mean, it would be kind of cool to save the heroes for once," Parker said with a shrug.

Ember took a deep breath. "We aren't going to get help from anyone at Glofiara, that much is clear. And if the headmistress is involved, we cannot tell a soul," she said as they began to walk away. "We'll have to find the proof for the Society ourselves."

"Imagine that—the remnants and a non-magic making sure something goes right. Otherwise, it's always people reminding us that we are only capable of destruction," Chloe said.

"It would be pretty awesome," Parker said, and then added, "But how do we do it?"

All three of them turned to Elias, who pushed his glasses up the crook of his nose. "What? I don't have answers all the time."

"Come on, you're like a walking library. Help us out," Parker said.

"Well, you and Ember figured out how to beat an exiled Ancient's puzzle and save us," Elias pointed out.

"I think the Gatekeeper was more lonely than anything," Chloe said.

"Can we not excuse an Ancient One's actions now?" Ember couldn't believe what she was saying. Until yesterday, she didn't even believe in the Ancient Ones. Until yesterday, her parents had been considered heroes. Now her world felt as if it were tilting on its axis.

Elias gazed down at his watch. "The library seems to be our best shot at finding answers, but Traces and other complex forms of magic are far beyond the scope of remnants, or our syllabus," Elias said. "So they won't be accessible to us."

Ember stopped walking. "But it might be available in the upper floors."

"You're forgetting something," Chloe said. "We don't have access to that part of the library. Did you forget how mad Mother Irene got last time?"

"I do remember," Ember said, staring at Parker. "Say, Parker. You might be able to help us out, right?"

"Only if you want to get us caught. My invisibility isn't exactly stable," Parker pointed out. "And in case you're forgetting, none of our powers actually work correctly, and Chloe doesn't have any. No offense."

"None taken," Chloe said. "In fact, I would like it better if we normalized talking about it."

"Right," Ember said. "I guess we might have to think of some other way." But for the life of her, she didn't have the faintest idea.

Chapter Twenty-One

FALLEN HEROES

That night, Chloe sat on Ember's bed until she let her inside. Ember could tell that Chloe was scared, and so was she. Who could they turn to when none of the actually-powerful adults listened to them? Who would they seek help from if the ones in charge were the evil ones?

Ember opened Chloe's comm-device to watch the news coverage of her parents coming out of the Society Grievance Redressal Council, or SGRC, as they called it. The reporters crowded around them with mics. Unlike Ember's brand-new one, Chloe's was a much older device, probably passed down from child to child.

"George and Rosetta Pearson, you just came out after a ten-hour interrogation. What is the stance of the Society on these accusations?"

Ember's dad looked like he had aged several years in a span of a few days. "We just want to stress the fact that we are innocent, and we're going to keep maintaining that fact. It's a misunderstanding that we hope to clear up as soon as possible."

"Is it true that you're going to trial in a few days?" one of the reporters asked.

Ember's father's face hardened. "I can't comment on that."

The reporter turned to the screen. "In a bizarre twist of fate, the two sorcerers, if found guilty, will be sent to the same place they sent their conquests before."

A headline flashed across the screen, almost blinding the two girls—FALLEN HEROES GEORGE AND ROSETTA PEARSON INVESTIGATED.

ONCE-CELEBRATED WHITE SORCERORS UNDER INVESTIGATION. NEWS OF THE CENTURY.

"You would think they would focus on the fact that one of the most notorious black sorcerers ever has escaped and try to find him. But no, they're bent on putting—on putting..." She trailed off, unable to get the rest of the words out.

Chloe turned off her comm-device. It was getting harder and harder for Ember to breathe. Tears stung at the corners of her eyes.

Ember curled up on her side while Chloe peered over her worriedly. "Are you okay, Ember?"

"I am," Ember lied. She wondered briefly if Summer was watching the news. If so, how was she taking it?

"We'll prove their innocence once we find whoever made the sigil," Chloe said.

"Yeah," Ember said, unconvinced. That night, Ember drifted off to an uneasy dream. There was a man who beckoned to her, asking for help. As soon as Ember walked up to him, he transformed into a terrifying, huge beast and caught her in his jaw.

Ember woke up drenched in sweat.

The next day, Ember could hardly drag herself out of bed to get to class. Snickers followed her past breakfast and into the hallways. People pointed at her and talked behind her back. Ember gritted her teeth as she walked. It took every ounce of her patience not to lash out.

Chloe looked at her worriedly. "Just try to ignore them."

"Well, well, well, how the mighty have fallen," Clarisse drawled, blocking Ember's entry into Magi-Physical science class.

"What is your problem?" Ember asked.

Clarisse narrowed her eyes. "You have so much nerve talking back when your parents are traitors."

"Nothing has been proven yet," Ember said, trying to keep her voice even.

Clarisse examined the bed of her nails. "You know, my parents always thought there was something odd about the Pearsons. We all know how people with too much power turn out, don't we?"

"Why are you blocking the entry into my class?" said a voice behind them. It was Professor Detteo. His brows were knitted together, and he seemed to be in a very foul mood. His appearance was disheveled, and there were deep bags under his eyes, as if he hadn't slept in a while.

Ember frowned, suddenly remembering that he had been late to the Main Hall when the headmistress had first announced that Mallorus had escaped. Ember watched him enter the class, his dark mantle swishing around him.

"Take your seats," he said curtly.

"Your time is up, Pearson," Clarisse said. "And Parker will be sorry he chose you losers over me."

Ember chose not to reply to her snark and sat down at one of the empty desks at the back. Today Professor Detteo taught them about the phenomenon of emergence, a.k.a. the first time that magi-users demonstrated power. It could be as early as two or as late as ten. Ideally, the child should have shown some presence of magic, but it isn't until the test of age that they're divided into remnants and Witchies.

Ember watched Professor Detteo as he went through the motions of the class. He had almost zero enthusiasm, as if he simply wanted to be done with his job and end the class. Ember realized that she had been so caught up with her theories, she had totally forgotten about Detteo. Of course, it would make sense to speak to him. Judging from his interaction with Nadie, they were friends. He was also the one conducting research on remnants.

Detteo had feelings for Nadie, so it was only fair that he would be affected by her absence. If she had left willingly, why would he look so disturbed? Which begged the question: did he know what had happened to her and perhaps was responsible for it?

"We need to talk to Professor Detteo," Ember said urgently.

Chloe frowned. "Why him?"

Ember briefly explained everything to her. "Oh, how could I have been so stupid? I should have spoken to him before."

"Relax, it's your first case and we're all new to this," Chloe reassured her. "It's a learning curve."

Ember nodded, but she knew she had committed a blunder. Now, it was time to fix it.

After the class ended, she was the first one out. She raced after the tall, wiry-framed man, calling out, "Professor! Professor Detteo."

He finally stopped walking and turned to face her. "Yes?"

"Professor, I was wondering about your research. I heard that you're doing some work related to isolation of magical—"

He cut her off mid-sentence. "Who told you that?"

Ember gulped. Nadie had made her promise not to tell him that she had taken the essence from Ember. "I read it somewhere."

Professor Detteo's eyes narrowed at her suspiciously. "Wait a minute. Did you steal from my lab?"

"What?" Ember spluttered. "What are you talking about?"

"Don't lie to me, girl," he said. Paranoia was evident on his face, and it scared Ember a little. He tried to reach for her, but she managed to dance out of his grip.

"You've got it all wrong."

"Leave me alone," Professor Detteo said, practically howling. With that, he turned on his heels and left.

Ember was aware of her classmates peering at her. She'd already had enough of everyone's attention. Instead of heading to her next class, she turned and fled.

Ember found herself in the temple. It was the middle of the day, so it was completely empty. She sat at the last pew, watching Mother Ethilenne's idol on the altar. Candles flickered at her feet—hundreds of them. The altar seemed to never run out of them.

"There you are," said a voice behind her. Elias was walking towards her. "We've been looking all over for you while you're in here sulking alone."

"I am not," Ember said.

"I thought you didn't believe in religion," Elias said.

"We met an Ancient One the other week, remember?" she said.

"Ah, the exiled brother," Elias said. According to Ethilenne's myth, she had two. Both had grown power-hungry over time and decided to steal her abilities.

"Do you think she's real?" Ember asked. "If so, why does she let bad things happen to good people?"

"I think Ethilenne is busy with her own problems and expects us to do the same for ourselves. You wouldn't want an Ancient One to run your life, would you?"

"A little guidance would be great right about now," Ember muttered. She had never felt so lost before. Considering the events of late, she couldn't even trust the adults. There were potential bad guys everywhere.

"You know what we're doing wrong? We're trying to fight an invisible enemy," Elias said.

"Since when is Mallorus invisible?"

"He isn't. What I mean is that none of us know much about him. That's because information about him has never come to light before. No books talk about him. He has been essentially wiped out of history. But your parents know something," Elias said.

"My parents don't talk about him or the past," Ember said.

"Maybe this time they might change their mind," Elias said.

Ember sighed. "I'll try."

That evening, she called her parents on the comm-device with the video on. She didn't expect them to pick up, but when they did, Ember felt her heart breaking. Both Rosetta and George looked worse for wear, bags under their eyes, their cheeks hollowed.

"Mom, Dad," Ember said.

"Ember," her father said, smiling faintly. "Just seeing you made my entire day."

Ember clutched the device hard. "They're saying horrible things about you and at school…" She trailed off, unable to get the rest out.

"I know how hard it must be for you, angel," her mother crooned softly. She was trying to be tough for Ember's sake; she could see that in her eyes. "Sometimes things start falling apart all around us, but we can always put them back together."

"Your mom's right," George said, adjusting his crooked glasses.

"But how did things get here?" Ember asked.

George and Rosetta exchanged a glance. "We don't know," her dad said, but Ember could tell there was something they weren't saying. "But it seems someone is trying to frame us."

"Is it somebody from Glofiara?" Ember asked. She almost said Headmistress Kinnera's name outright but didn't want to risk it.

Her father frowned. "What are you talking about?"

"Uh, never mind. What were you saying? Did you figure out who it is?"

"Nothing is clear as of yet, but the Society seems determined to punish us," George said. "Perhaps it didn't help our cause that we were all the way out in the wilderness of Peru when Mallorus escaped and news got to us quite late."

"Do you think someone wanted that to happen?" Ember asked.

"That's ridiculous," her mother said. "All our missions are signed off by the Society, and why would they try to frame us?"

"Can you find out who approved your mission?" Ember asked.

"We'll try, but those records are sealed by magical laws. Technically, if the files aren't released, we won't be able to talk about it at court."

Ember's jaw dropped. "That's unfair."

"We know, kiddo, and trust me, we have the best team with us trying to fix this," Rosetta said.

"What about Mallorus, though?" Ember said. "Could he or one of his followers have planned it?"

George looked at her sharply. "Ember, I told you to stay away from all that."

"Please, I'm old enough to know," Ember said.

"He's been in prison all this while. His followers disbanded after he was banished. Some of his generals were put in there with him, but as far as we know, only he got out," Rosetta said.

"What about Mallorus himself?" Ember said. "How did he get to be so powerful?"

They exchanged another glance. "He was one of the most powerful sorcerers of our time, but he always thirsted for more. Remember one thing, Ember: the more power you seek, the more influence it has on you. It can corrupt your soul, as it did to Mallorus."

A shiver passed through Ember at her dad's words. She remembered the pond of illusions whispering and promising her great powers.

"Why did he get so greedy?"

"Not many people know about this, but Mallorus was once identified as the Chosen One," George said.

Ember gasped. "The Chosen One?"

Her mom nodded. "The diviners chose him themselves, plucked him from some orphanage where he had been abandoned. He showed great powers when he was barely five."

"Five years?" Ember asked.

"Five months," George clarified.

"There was a prophecy that talked of a great Darkness befalling us," Rosetta said. "The diviners chose Mallorus to combat the Darkness. But it never came to pass. Mallorus went mad with grief for something he never had. He could never become the hero."

"The irony was, he turned into the villain that the prophecy warned us about," George said.

Ember gasped. "But why does nobody talk about this?"

"It was swept under the rug, as it was an error of grave magnitude. The diviners never make a mistake like this—" George said.

"But this time they did," Rosetta finished. "The Society would be disbanded if the rest of the magic community ever found out."

Ember was still reeling from the information. *That's why he went bad?*

George nodded. "I know how it might sound to you, but Mallorus spent his entire life training for a destiny that was snatched away. It was too much for him."

"And then the massacre at Branshaw happened," Rosetta said.

"What's that?" Ember said.

"We cannot tell you. You're too young."

Ember didn't push them on it. She would circle back to it later. "But what puts him apart from the rest of us? Why is he so powerful?"

"Because he can get inside your head, find your deepest secrets and deepest pain, and use them against you," Rosetta said.

"Not only that, it was extremely hard to track him because of his incredible ability to Shift," George said.

"But that's illegal magic, right?" Ember asked, her eyes widening. Suddenly, everything became clear to her. "You mean he can shift into animals, right?"

Before either of them could answer, someone threw open the door.

"Ember, we're not supposed to be in contact with anyone from the outside world. We borrowed this comm-device from our friend as ours was confiscated. We don't want to get her into trouble lest anybody finds it on us. We need to go."

"But Dad, I have—"

"It'll be okay, kiddo. Take care of your sister. We love you," her mom said. She glanced briefly at the door again before turning to her. "Everything will be fine." With that, the line went dark.

Chapter Twenty-Two

A Ghostly Specter

When Chloe came into the room, Ember wasn't crying anymore. The conversation with her parents had set off something inside of her. Chloe looked confused. "What's wrong?"

"That day in the forest, it wasn't the pond. It was never the pond," Ember said.

Chloe's brows furrowed. "What are you talking about?"

"It was Mallorus," Ember said. The truth had dawned on her the moment her parents told her about his powers along with the other revelation. "He was the one manipulating us. It was his voice we heard."

Chloe's mouth dropped open. "So he *is* here."

Ember nodded, a shiver passing down her spine. It wasn't just the Order of Shadows that Nadie had encountered in the forest; it was

Mallorus. "That's his ability. He's a Spirit user, like Elias, but of the worst sort. He can mess with our heads."

Chloe clapped her hand to her mouth. "Oh no. That means he tried to kill us."

"Or at least get us out of his way," Ember said grimly. "Which means we must have been closing in on him."

"That's right," Chloe said.

"And not only that—the animal that Nadie had been chasing, it was him, as well. Mallorus is a Shifter."

"Dear Ethilenne," Chloe said. "Poor Nadie fell for his trap."

"That's how he must have been hiding out there in the forest," Ember said, pacing the room. "But nobody will believe us."

"We need to talk to the boys," Chloe said. "They might be able to help."

During dinner, they got the table at the farthest corner of the room, away from everyone else. Ember was all but a social pariah now. People kept tittering behind her, but she didn't care anymore. She was going to hunt down Mallorus and make him pay for whatever he did to Nadie, and for what he was doing to her parents.

Parker and Elias slipped into the table opposite to her. "Chloe told me you found something," Elias said.

"I did," Ember said quietly. She told them everything she had learned from her parents. The story had started to fall into place.

"So Mallorus must have been broken out by someone here, the same one who drew the sigil," Elias said. "Once they brought him here, he shifted into an injured Tekkow so that people would be none the wiser."

"The patrolling warlocks wouldn't bother with a forest creature," Chloe said. "He would be left alone to come and go."

"The Zoo-Keep told me that he released the beast back into the forest," Ember said. "If only he had realized what the Tekkow actually was."

"Wait, you spoke to Travis?" Parker asked. "When?"

"Last week," Ember said. "After he came back."

Parker nodded. "I don't remember seeing a Tekkow there, but it must have been after my shift ended."

"The animal chewed a part of his leg off," Ember said.

"Poor man," Chloe said, clucking her tongue.

"Back to the trouble at hand," Elias said, his voice dropping as he leaned forward. "What are we going to do about Mallorus and his fanatic followers? There might even be multiple."

Parker shook his head. "Going up against Mallorus is a death wish, right? We'll never make it."

"What did your parents have to say about defeating Mallorus?" Elias asked.

"I don't know, the call got disconnected before I could ask, and my parents wouldn't have told me anyway. They don't want me anywhere near him. But we can't sit here and do nothing," Ember said.

"We have to get access to the upper floors of the library," Elias said. "Then we can figure out the deal with Traces and who drew the sigil in the forest. Once we know the identity of that person, we'll have the proof we need that Glofiara is compromised. We won't even have to deal with Mallorus."

"Elias is right," Ember said. "That sounds like a logical plan."

"And here I thought we were going up against Mallorus head-on—three remnants and a non-magic, what a good team we make," Parker said sarcastically.

"I hope you got that out of your system, because there's work to be done," Ember said, rolling her eyes.

"What makes you think we'll be able to find the answers that people at the Society missed? People who are more powerful than we'll ever be."

"They're not looking in the right place," Ember said. "We have to at least try."

"So what's the plan?" Parker asked. All three sets of eyes turned to him. "Well, it kind of entirely hinges on you," Chloe said. "You're the Invisible one."

Parker laughed. "I can hardly stay invisible. Why don't you get your sister to bring you whatever you need? She has access to the upper levels, right?"

Ember bit her tongue. "Summer is a stickler for rules. She'll never allow it."

"What's the alternative?" Chloe asked. "Parker's just going to end up busting himself."

An idea suddenly crossed Ember's mind. "You don't have to be invisible—I mean, you do, but only for a short period of time."

"And how's that going to help?" Parker asked with a frown.

"You will create a distraction for us and then get out," Ember said. The others gathered around Ember as she explained the plan.

The next day, Parker was the first to stride into the library. He was invisible, of course, but like a ghostly specter, he kept coming in and out of view.

Mother Irene was dusting a shelf nearby. She looked up just as Parker disappeared again. A few students were sitting around the long wood table studying. "Did you see something?" Mother Irene said, her voice sounding like chalk against a blackboard.

A few children shook their heads.

Just then, Parker darted, just in her vision. "There it is," Mother Irene cried. She beat the air with the duster as if she were doing a crazy dance. When the duster clattered out of her hand, she whipped around to face the other side.

Ember and Chloe took the opportunity to start climbing the stairs. Ember glanced down at the floor once. Parker materialized behind one of the bookshelves and winked up at her.

"Come on," Chloe said. Ember hastily climbed the rest of the steps. Plush carpet greeted them at the top. There were several levels, each lined with thousands—if not millions—of books.

Ember gaped up at the ceiling. Books stretched as far as the eye could see. "How are we even going to figure out what books we need?"

"Look there," Chloe said, pointing at something in the distance. There were three vacuum-like tubes that seemed to pass through all the levels. The material was opaque, so Ember couldn't really see what was going on inside. There was a buzzer attached. "I guess we just tell it what we want."

"Just like that?" Ember asked.

Chloe cleared her throat as she walked up to the tube. She was poised and confident, and Ember realized this was where Chloe felt like she truly belonged, amongst books—something she dearly loved. "Hmm, let's see. We need a book on dark magic."

At first, nothing happened, but then a clatter of books fell down the spine of the tube, and it kept on coming like gushing water. "Wait, wait stop," Chloe said hastily. Ember helped her put the books that had come out into the other dispensary, the one that appeared to collect the read books.

"Okay, we need a book or two on Traces," Ember said.

Two books swooshed down the tube. The first one was a leather-bound edition of a book called *Tracing Magic and Evolution through the Ages,* and the second was called *The Beginner's Guide to Your Inner Eye.*

"Why are the titles so cheesy though?" Chloe said, turning one over in her hand.

"Tracing magic to help find something," Ember called out. Two more books appeared. *The Practical Guide to Traces* and *Isolating Your Psyche*.

"I think we have all we need," Ember said. She picked up the books and turned to leave just as footsteps approached. Chloe and Ember froze.

Summer's voice echoed ahead before she actually appeared around the bend. She was with Talis. "I don't know why you're picking a fight with me."

"I just want to know why you're covering for her. I know you don't like her," Talis was saying. Ember's heart sank. She took Chloe's hand and tugged her to the back of one of the bookshelves and hid there.

Summer came into view. "Careful, she's my sister."

"Not that you cared about that much," Talis said. "Remember when we used to go to your room and you insisted that you had no siblings? You never let us meet her."

Ember's stomach sank. She knew none of Summer's friends except Xander, and that had been by mistake. Once, when she was eight, she had wandered out of her room. Summer had seemed upset at her for some reason, and Ember didn't really understand why until now.

"I was a kid. I made stupid decisions, but that's all in the past and—" Summer broke off. Ember wasn't fast enough to hide. She met her sister's gaze across the aisle. Summer sucked in a breath before letting it out.

Talis frowned at her. "What are you looking at?"

Before she could turn around and catch the two girls, Summer gripped her elbow. "Come on."

Talis tried to free herself of her grip. "What is wrong with you?"

"Nothing," Summer said. "I just wanted to take a quick look at one of the shelves at the back. Someone was telling me one of the tubes isn't working."

Talis scoffed. "So what? It's not our job to fix it."

"Let's take a look anyway. We have the apprentice exam coming up soon," Summer said. She glanced at Ember, who understood that they only had a short window to escape before Talis caught her. Ember nodded stiffly. She didn't really know how to feel about Summer. But Ember knew that the feeling of unwantedness she had experienced since childhood wasn't just in her head. Her family always knew there was something different about her, something broken. Her magic never worked right, no matter how hard she practiced. They probably wanted to get her test of age over with as soon as possible. After all, it would just tell them what they already knew. And then she got an official diagnosis—she was a remnant.

In the magic world, *remnancy* wasn't classified as a disease in the strictest sense. It would be more analogous to a genetic condition.

Summer and Talis disappeared to the back, and their voices faded away.

Ember texted Parker on her comm-device to let him know that they were on their way down. Chloe put the books in her bag, and the two of them slowly tiptoed to the staircase. Thankfully, they didn't run into anybody else there.

They waited by the banister for Parker as he continued to distract Mother Irene. A few books were scattered on the ground, and more seemed to come off the shelves for no apparent reason. Irene seemed almost hysterical at that point. "There's a poltergeist in here," she said. She hit one of the students who was studying and narrowly missed hitting Parker. Once Ember and Chloe tumbled out of the library, they signaled for Parker to follow.

They raced out to the hallway and waited for Parker to catch up. But when he didn't come out after several minutes, Ember knew something was wrong. She started to retrace her steps just as Parker was escorted out of the library by Summer and Talis, led by Headmistress Kinnera.

"Oh no," Chloe said under her breath as they watched from the back of the shelf.

"I've found your alleged poltergeist, Irene," Kinnera said drily. "As for you, Parker, I don't think just a stern word is going to do this time."

Parker hung his head and nodded. Before Ember could do anything, they walked him away.

Chapter Twenty-Three

SOMETHING TO HIDE

"We knew there was a chance of this happening. Parker knew it too," Elias said. "We spoke about this last night."

"You did?" Ember said. "And he still went ahead with it?"

Elias sighed. "That's the thing about our powers, right? They're unstable and act against us."

"So what happened?" Ember asked. Elias was supposed to be in the reading section, keeping an eye out for both Parker and the girls.

"After you guys left, Parker tried to get away, but he accidentally bumped into a student and revealed himself."

Guilt ate away at Ember. It was because of her reckless plan that Parker was caught. "He didn't return to bed last night," Elias said, which made Ember feel much worse. He wasn't in any classes either.

"Do you think they did something to him?" Chloe asked worriedly. They were huddled up next to each other in the courtyard outside. It was an overcast day with distant rumbling clouds.

"I honestly don't know," Elias said. "I hope they don't suspend him. If you think about it, it was just a silly prank."

Chloe and Ember nodded in agreement. But Ember wouldn't put anything past the severe headmistress.

"Did you get the books we wanted?" Elias asked.

Ember nodded. That was the only bright spot in the otherwise dull afternoon. The three of them mourned the loss of a member. It almost felt like a part of them had been cut out.

"I think it's probably for the best to leave him out of it," Ember said, tracing her big toe over the concrete. "I don't want to get him into any more trouble than he is now."

Elias nodded. "I'll go through the books and get to you with notes," Elias said. "Together, we are going to crack the mystery."

"But even if we manage to get everything right, what about the forest itself? Won't it try to attack us like last time?" Chloe asked. "I don't want to accidentally end up in an exiled Ancient's dimension again. We may not be able to escape a second time."

"Valid question," Elias said. "You know, I never really understood why or how the forest specifically targets only remnants. Maybe it's programmed the other way around."

"What do you mean?" Ember asked, frowning.

"Maybe it's enchanted not to attack the instructors or the other staff. In simple words, people who aren't remnants," Elias said. "It's called selective magic. A powerful diviner along with a sorcerer might have been able to do it."

"So the myths about the forest?"

"Probably generated by word of mouth," Elias said.

"But the Gatekeeper was real," Ember pointed out.

"Maybe he wasn't part of the plan. Magic is unpredictable that way," Elias said. "Besides, mortals can hardly decide where an Ancient One lives. But from what I can tell, the forest basically acts as a pocket into Timonus' realm. It's purely coincidental."

"If you're right, that's probably how Nadie must have been able to go into the forest," Ember said.

"That's how Mallorus must have been hiding in the forest, too," Elias said.

"With the help of somebody at Glofiara," Ember finished.

"Correct," Elias said.

"But how do we figure out exactly how the non-remnants go in there?" Ember said. "Besides, what about Chloe?"

"Oh, I wasn't attacked," Chloe said off-handedly. "I just wandered off, trying to find you guys, and the next thing I knew, Mallorus was hijacking me towards the pond."

Ember blinked. "So the forest has a flaw. It can recognize remnants, but it can't recognize full-fledged magic users or non-magics."

Elias shook his head. "No, that's not it. The trees might be sentient, but their decision-making capability isn't that evolved. They're alerted of our presence some other way."

Absent-mindedly, Ember looked down. She gasped as realization dawned on her. "The talismans!"

Elias nodded excitedly. "That must be it. Remember how Headmistress Kinnera specifically told us never to take it off?"

"Chloe wasn't attacked because she didn't have a talisman."

"Right," Chloe said, nodding enthusiastically.

"The talismans must act like a resicurse," Elias said, looking at the talisman, fascinated. "They were never just to keep our powers in check."

"They are to keep *us* in check!" Ember said.

"What's a resicurse?" Chloe asked.

"It's like a complex magic code written to act as a repellent spell or enchantment. Well, long story short, this is why the forest reacts so violently to our presence," said Elias.

"So all those stories about the forest trying to keep us out—well, trapped at Glofiara?" Ember said.

"Lies propagated to keep us in line. I mean, I've heard of people trying to escape Glofiara. This place isn't exactly ideal. Maybe that's why they spread the rumor."

"And put the talismans on us like we're sheep to be herded," Ember said, with growing anger inside her.

"What about any trespassing humans, though?" Chloe asked. "They wouldn't be wearing any talisman."

"They aren't able to see through the glamor. I just can't wrap my head around the wrongness of it all."

"Well, they think we are a menace to society," Ember said. "Even my parents, they couldn't wait to dump me out here and forget all about me."

"I'm sure that's not true. The remnants are here to be trained to use—"

"Do you really believe all of that? Two months of the semester have passed, yet we don't have the first clue how to control our powers," Ember said. "They just want to suppress our abilities and move on to the next so that the remnants aren't any more trouble."

Elias finally nodded. "I guess you have a point." He rose from the bench. "I'll go get started on reading the books. We have a long way uphill ahead of us."

"Good luck getting through those," Ember said.

"Can I help?" Chloe chimed in. "I'm pretty good at reading too."

Elias hesitated, and at first it appeared that he would turn her down, but then he nodded. "Okay, we can work on them together. We'll get more done in a shorter period of time."

Chloe clapped her hands in glee and excitedly followed Elias. Ember smiled after them; however, it faded when Summer walked up to her. Ember picked up her bag and started to leave.

"I know that you sneaking in that library while the boy created a distraction was no coincidence," she said.

Ember paused. "I don't know what you mean."

"You're up to something," Summer said, before her expression softened. "Come on, tell me what's going on. I can help."

At first, Ember thought she would come clean, but then she remembered what Talis had said about Summer's feelings towards her. "No, you can't."

"Ember, please," Summer said. "After what happened with Mom and Dad, it's important, now more than ever, to stick together."

Ember shook her head. "You can't help me, not when you don't even want me around." She took off before Summer could say anything else. Ember felt on the edge of tears again. Her body was beginning to burn. She didn't realize when she had run past the empty corridors and found herself in a new, smaller courtyard.

"Strange," she murmured. Ember had never been here before.

A few feet away, she saw two figures steeped in shadows. Headmistress Kinnera stepped forward, which caught Ember by surprise. What was she doing here alone?

"Did you do what I asked?" she was saying.

"Yes, but I'm still not convinced it's going to work, Mother," a familiar voice replied. Ember's brows knitted as she tried to figure out who it was. The Headmistress had a son? But who? Her mind was reeling from the revelation.

"Fool, we can't afford attention on us, not when we are this close to having a breakthrough," Kinnera said, sounding almost angry.

"I'll try my best, but I don't think they will allow it, Mother," said the other voice.

The headmistress started to say something but stiffened. "It seems that we have an eavesdropper," she said.

Ember hid behind one of the tall columns. There was no way she saw her.

"Miss Pearson," the headmistress called. "Please step out."

Ember swallowed hard.

"Don't make me repeat myself," she said.

Ember reluctantly came out of her hiding place and walked up to the headmistress. There was no other person in sight. Ember thought that it could have been Professor Detteo, but from such a great distance, she really couldn't be sure. Besides, what were they whispering about? And most importantly—they were related? Ember tried to recall their interactions at the school and came up with nothing. They were never seen together, much less conversing.

"What are you doing out here alone?" Headmistress Kinnera asked. "Don't you have your class?"

"We had a pop quiz and the instructor let us go early," Ember said.

"Hmm, do you enjoy exploring new places, or does it have more to do with your habit of eavesdropping?"

"I wasn't—"

"Don't deny it, Miss Pearson," Headmistress Kinnera said. "One of your dear friends, Parker, was discovered doing mischief in the library. You wouldn't know anything about that, would you?"

Ember swallowed. She had half a mind to come clean, but that would mean confessing the truth about why they were there in the first place and would get both Chloe and Elias in trouble.

"No, ma'am," she said. "I have no idea."

"He's a troublemaker, but it seems rather odd to me that he would do that for no reason at all," Kinnera continued.

Ember stood there, feeling the balloon of guilt slowly taking over her. "I don't know."

"He has been punished appropriately, as troublemakers are," Headmistress Kinnera said. "But don't think I don't see what you Misveez are trying to do."

Ember blinked in shock. "Excuse me?"

Even Headmistress Kinnera seemed to be caught off-guard. She cleared her throat. "You cannot deceive me, Miss Pearson. The next time you mess up, I'll make sure you are out of this school before you can blink. That'll put an end to all the ambitions that you've cooked up, because I hope you know what happens to children who are kicked out of Glofiara. They become pariahs. You might want to keep that in mind."

All Ember could think was, *She has something to hide.*

Parker was there at dinner. At first, Ember couldn't believe what she was seeing. She walked up to him, but he wouldn't even look at her. "Parker," she called but got no response. It was like he couldn't hear her.

"Move, loser," Clarisse's snooty voice said, coming up from behind Ember and almost knocking the tray of food she was carrying. As Ember watched, Clarisse sat down next to Parker and draped a hand over him. "Dear Parker has finally come to his senses. You can take yourself elsewhere."

Irritation flared through Ember. "Touch me again," she warned, "and you'll sorely regret it."

Clarisse laughed, the sound cruel. "You do not scare me, Firestarter. You're the pariah—the daughter of traitors. Turns out your parents were never heroes in the first place."

"That's enough, Clar," Parker said. He had gone back to calling her by his affectionate nickname. "I don't want any trouble at dinner."

Clarisse ruffled his hair gently. "Of course, sweetpea."

Ember almost gagged. Parker had ditched them for good? Clarisse and Parker were a thing now? Gross.

She walked away from the table without another word. Elias never showed up at dinner, so Chloe and Ember ate together. The whispers had faded into quiet din, and people were no longer pointing fingers at her.

Ember's comm-device pinged with a text. It was from Summer. *The Pearson trial is scheduled for next week. The hearing will be televised on EtherTV.*

Chloe and Ember exchanged a glance. They both knew what this meant. They had only a few days to prove the Pearson's innocence.

Chapter Twenty-Four

DOGAMAR DUTY

That night, Ember found it hard to sleep. Chloe was up too, reading a book.

"Thinking about your parents?" Chloe asked.

Ember nodded, running a hand over Toasty, who was sound asleep, curled up beside her belly. At least one of them didn't have anything to worry about.

Ember opened her comm-device and scrolled through the pictures in the gallery of her family.

Both the girls fell silent for a while before Ember said, "Do you miss yours?"

Chloe shrugged. "I've never met them."

Ember sat up straighter on her bed. "What do you mean?"

"I grew up in foster care under the Conservation Society. When my family noticed that I didn't display any sort of power as I grew up, they thought it better to send me away as soon as possible. They had other children to take care of, and resources were stretched thin at the home."

"Chloe," Ember breathed. She couldn't stand her elder sister most of the time and hated the way her family treated her—always walking on eggshells around her—but she would rather have a messy family than not have one at all. She understood the importance of family, now more than ever. "I'm so sorry. I had no idea."

"It's fine," Chloe said with a watery smile. "You can't miss someone you've never met, right? Besides, I have this." She held up the video-recorder. "It was left with me at the Conservation Society doorstep. That's the way they knew I came from magic." Nobody from the human community would have access to the Conservation Society, they wouldn't even be able to even see it. It kept changing its appearance and location, and much like Glofiara and the other magic-training schools, it was cloaked with a thick layer of charm blanket.

"And they never found out who left you there?" Ember asked. Poor Chloe. She didn't have any idea who she really was and where she came from.

"No," Chloe said, shaking her head. "I mean, they tried. They put out posters, they even tried to get me adopted, but no one would take a non-magic for fear of the stigma it would bring. Don't get me wrong—my foster parents never treated me badly. They were indifferent, but only because they had so many children to take care of. They thought that when I was grown enough, Glofiara would be the best place for me so that I could take my place in the human society, where I belong."

"Don't let anyone say you don't belong here, you get that?" Ember said fiercely.

Chloe smiled. Even in the dark, Ember could tell she was on the verge of tears. "All I've ever wanted is to belong."

Ember got off her bed, almost sending Toasty to the floor. "You do," Ember said, sitting on the bed beside her. "You belong here."

Chloe's comm-device began to buzz. She frowned as she looked around for it in her pile of pillows.

"Who's messaging so late at night?" Ember wondered. They got their answer when Chloe finally managed to locate her device. It was a flip version, at least a three-to-four-year-old model with lots of scratches. The side of the paneling was bruised. Ember thought about Chloe's weird mismatch of clothes. Maybe they weren't intentional; maybe those clothes were all she had.

"It's Elias," Chloe murmured, reading the message. "He wants to meet."

"But it's almost midnight," Ember said. They had already lost a member, and she didn't want to get the others into further trouble. The headmistress's threat loomed over her head. Would she make good on her word and kick her out?

"He says it's really important and that he found something in the books," Chloe said.

Ultimately, curiosity won over. Ember zipped up her hoodie before stepping towards the door. "We have to be careful," she told Chloe.

A loud croaking caught her attention. It was Toasty, and he was blocking their way. Ember could almost swear that she saw him scowling.

"I think he feels left out," Chloe said, looking at the toad sympathetically. The toad croaked louder as if affirming her words.

"Toasty, don't be a brat," Ember said. "We can't take you."

"Yeah, it's not safe for you out there. We aren't supposed to have pets," Chloe said.

"This place sucks," Ember muttered, but then something dawned on her. Maybe Toasty felt the same way. When was the last time he had stepped out of the room except to go out to the ledge and get his business done?

Ember knelt on the floor and motioned to him to leap up to her shoulders. Toasty croaked happily before bounding up her arm. He hid himself behind the blue tips of Ember's hair.

"You're taking him?" Chloe asked.

"I just realized that I've been keeping him a prisoner here," Ember said. "How is that any different than what Glofiara is doing to us?"

"I know that everything that Glofiara stands for seems wrong to you, but it has given me something I never had before—a home and a family. Maybe once I graduate, I'll actually be useful by serving the human society."

Ember stayed silent. She was still hoping that she would transfer to Zanith. But it didn't necessarily mean that she would have to break her friendship with Chloe just because she was going to a different school. Besides, Chloe seemed to actually like living at Glofiara.

The two girls and a rather fat toad headed out into the night. They were careful not to turn their Glo-Torches to a high setting. They followed the sandstone floors down a row of corridors and headed towards the inner sanctum where the school classrooms were.

"Elias said he found one of the classrooms on the third floor unlocked," Chloe said. "He asked us to meet him there. Third door on the right."

"There it is," Ember said, walking up to the door. "But it's shut tight. Look." Toasty croaked in affirmation.

"We'll just have to try to catch their attention," Chloe said, trying to push the door open.

"Who is that?" came Elias's voice.

"It's us," Chloe said.

"You have to answer the secret code to get inside," Elias said.

Ember rolled her eyes. "Don't be ridiculous. Let us in."

The door opened after a brief rumbling. Elias appeared on the other side, his hair a mess and his glasses askew. Ember wondered if he had even eaten anything.

He looked sheepish. "Sorry, I guess I was just trying to channel the Gatekeeper."

"If I see that guy in twenty years, it'll be too soon," Ember said.

Elias grinned.

"Why didn't you come down for dinner?" Chloe asked. She took out something from her bag. "Here's a sandwich for you."

"You're so sweet, Chloe," said someone from the back of the room. Ember and Chloe gasped in unison while Parker grinned in response. He was perched on top of a tall desk, his feet dangling in front of him. They hadn't noticed him because of how dark it was.

"Parker," Ember gasped. "What are you doing here?"

Toasty the Toad took that moment to reveal himself. He leaped from Ember's shoulder and launched himself at Elias—or, more specifically, at the sandwich that he had in his hand.

Elias yelped in surprise and fell to the ground.

"Toasty!" Ember said in a reprimanding tone. "Bad toad."

Parker leaped off the desk and jogged to them. "No way, you're secretly hiding contraband here?"

"It's just Toasty, my pet toad," Ember said reluctantly as she scooped him up off the floor.

"Awesome," Parker said, watching Toasty in barely disguised fascination.

"No, not awesome. He basically just tried to maul me—or my sandwich," Elias said, shaking his head as he sat up.

"Come here, little one," Parker said, his tone gentle and coaxing.

Ember stared at him. "Wait, you aren't freaked out like Elias?"

Toasty jumped from Ember's arm into Parker's. "Are you kidding me? I told you, I love animals. That means all of them." He cradled Toasty in his arms, who croaked mournfully, probably because he was unable to steal the food from Elias.

"And where have you been hiding this little hellion?" Elias asked.

Ember shrugged. "He's just been in my room. I'm telling you, he's harmless."

"I agree," Parker said. He seemed to already have bonded with Toasty, which made Ember roll her eyes. Her pet seemed to like her friends more than her, which reminded her....

"What are you doing here?" Ember asked. "I thought you weren't talking to us anymore."

Elias and Parker exchanged a loaded glance. "I wanted to talk to you before but couldn't because of Clarisse. The headmistress told her to keep an eye on me. I'm sorry for being rude to you before."

"So you don't hate me?" she said, relieved.

"Why would I hate you?" Parker asked, his brows knitted together. "I admit I've done some things in the past that I'm really not very proud of, and I would like to move past all of that."

"Me too," Ember agreed.

"Now, if we are done with the emotional arc, can we focus on the problem at hand?" Elias asked, pointing at the stack of books.

"What did you find out?" Chloe asked.

Elias took a deep breath and walked up to the board as if he were an instructor preparing to teach a class. "I read all about Traces to figure out how Mallorus or one of his followers might have framed your parents, but there's still a few things I don't understand."

"What?" Ember asked. She was practically on the edge of her seat.

"The Dogamar team uses the specialized fingerprint system to identify a Trace. The closest analogy to it would be human DNA. As soon as they put the Trace in the system, boom, the markers light up."

"I heard Clarisse saying that they found it to be a sixty-five percent match, which is pretty incriminating considering the amount they had for analyzing," said Parker.

"How did she hear that?" Ember said. She was pretty sure it wasn't in the news.

"She has an uncle who works at the Society," Parker said. "But I agree that we can't simply go off her words. She can be pretty biased."

Ember stayed silent.

"In order to frame your parents, either Mallorus or one of his followers would have had to extract the essence. It's a voluntary process or..." He trailed off.

"Or?" Chloe said.

"Dead," Elias said. "But your parents aren't, which means that they got the essence voluntarily."

Ember shook her head. "That's impossible. They must have collected it from someplace else."

"Well, they got it from somewhere," Elias said.

"Wait," Ember said as an epiphany struck her. "You said it was like human DNA, right? So that means he could have technically gotten it from me or Summer?"

"Why would your sister break Mallorus out?" Parker asked.

"She didn't," Ember said. "But I think I did."

Chapter Twenty-Five

A Cloaked Figure

The three gaped at Ember. Parker was the first one to speak up. "You did what?"

Ember shook her head. "I mean, I didn't do it, not intentionally anyway, but I think I might have helped, and involuntarily put Nadie's life at risk, as well."

"Explain everything or my mind is going to explode," Elias said.

Ember took a deep breath. "Nadie told me about an experimental process that Professor Detteo was working on that could theoretically stabilize a remnant's power. She said Detteo was looking for test subjects but he didn't want to be biased, and Nadie didn't want me to do it but I kind of forced her into it despite the fact that I'm not seventeen yet, which is the official age of consent." Ember was aware that she was blabbering by that point.

"Wait, why would you agree to that?" Elias asked.

"She wants to get into Zanith," Chloe said. "She told me the very day she moved in at Glofiara."

Ember's cheeks smarted. "I just...I was very motivated."

"Wait, is that what I saw when I came in that day in her office?" Parker asked. "Nadie was extracting your essence?"

"Yep," Ember said. "I didn't want you to blab."

"I wouldn't have," Parker said.

"I know that now," Ember said.

"What happened then?" Elias asked.

"Professor Detteo saw me with Nadie. Nadie told him that I was one of her favorites. He might have motivated her to get the extract from me. When she realized that he manipulated her, he tried to hurt her and she disappeared," Ember said. "Maybe he even used the excuse of the injured animal to lure her out. Everybody knows how kind-hearted she is."

"And her penchant for taking in strays," Parker said. Ember nodded. She was one of them.

Elias was frowning. "That seems like a stretch. You think Professor Detteo is the one helping Mallorus?"

"Wait until you hear what I saw today," Ember said. She gave them a short rundown of the conversation she had overheard the headmistress having with Detteo. "It would make sense for them both to work together to hide the news of Nadie's disappearance. Because they're family."

"And no one would know," Parker said. "I can see that happening. Besides, it does seem rather odd to me how the headmistress seems to be fixated on us. She's waiting for us to mess up."

"Probably because we keep getting into trouble," Elias pointed out.

"I know it might be a little hard for you to wrap your mind around, but sometimes the people in charge can be the bad guys," Parker said.

"She also called us something—I think it was the Misveez?" Ember said.

"Wait," Elias said. "Where have I heard that word?"

"Can we focus on the present, please?" Chloe said. "We know the problem, but how do we approach its solution?"

"Good question," Elias said. "Traces work backward when it comes to spiritual magic. We can use things like belongings, or something even as tiny as a strand of hair to track it. Really, I can go on and on about how intricately science is related to magic."

"Just get to the point," Parker said.

"He already made it," Chloe said. "Elias is a spiritual magic—a clairvoyant. He can use the symbols we found at the forest to track its owner."

Excitement buzzed through Ember as she finally understood what he was trying to tell them. Elias scratched his nose. "Well, it's all theoretical, and my powers are pretty unpredictable."

"But it is still possible," Ember said.

"Probability says so," Elias said. "But solid numbers work for full-fledged magic users, not remnants. My visions are always muddled; I can never separate or streamline the past from the future. That's why clairvoyants are not used in investigative magic anymore. Even the veterans make mistakes."

Ember remembered what her parents had told her about Mallorus, how the Society had created evil by making him believe that he was the savior. "We can still try," Ember said.

Toasty, who had been silent all this while, croaked in affirmation. Elias took off his glasses and rubbed his forehead. "Well, I suppose we have to, now that the toad says so."

The children spent the next couple of days meeting after midnight. Summer, Talis, and Xander still patrolled every night, but the security had grown lax in the weeks since Mallorus had escaped. It was almost like everybody had forgotten about that. The Pearson trial became the focal point of everybody's interest.

"I, for one, can't wait for justice to prevail," Clarisse said in the line to grab lunch, loud enough for Ember to hear. She ignored it, but Ember knew that she was running out of time.

They only had a couple of days before the trial began, and Elias was nowhere close to mastering his technique. They would hide their clothes, chocolates, etc. in different parts of the school for Elias to find simply by touching them. It was like playing a game of hide-and-seek, but Elias only had his visions to guide him.

Chloe had her video-cam out for all of these attempts.

"Are you recording everything?" Elias asked, looking particularly annoyed after his discovery that one of his favorite books had been stuck on a dead end.

"I'll have something to look at when we go home for winter break," Chloe said with a shrug.

The three older remnants looked at each other. They all loved Chloe. Who wouldn't? She was adorable.

By the third day, Elias had managed to find a couple of things, but he was nowhere close to an expert.

"We've only got one shot when we go into the forest," Ember said.

Elias, who was panting after a particularly grueling expedition of finding Toasty, said, "I don't know, Em. We are talking about actual dark magic. I don't think I'll hold up against it."

They were on the ground floor and were on their way back to the dorm after another unsatisfactory session. Ember didn't want to pressure Elias. He was just a kid, and this was way above his pay grade.

Ember was feeling more and more dejected by the second. She was desperate for something, anything. There were less than forty-eight hours till the clock ticked to zero. The evidence was overwhelming. Her parents would never win unless she did something.

"Guys," Chloe said.

Ember's ears perked up at the sound of distant rumbling. "What is that?"

"Sounds like something is growing closer—like a bee or something," Parker said. He was wrong.

Ember turned on her heel just as a tall wave of water hurtled towards them. "Guys," she said. "Run."

She grabbed Chloe by the hand and made sure Toasty was perched on top of her shoulders before taking off. They were in one of the blind corridors with one exit, and they had no choice but to keep running as the water chased them.

"I've never seen anything like that," Parker said. "We can't outrun it."

No sooner had he said those words than the water gushed forward, swallowing the children in its current. Ember tried to swim blindly, but the momentum of the wave proved too much for her.

There was a ledge a few feet away. Ember tried to swim towards it, but the current swept her away. It eventually deposited her on the lawn outside. Ember sat up as she coughed out water. She was transported back to the time when Mallorus had almost drowned them in the pond. Was it him again?

Confused shrieks echoed down from the upper floors as the dorms flooded and the water filled the hallway. There was no way it could have gone up so far if not for some kind of powerful magical intervention. Ember's friends were nowhere to be seen.

She got Toasty out of her jacket. As soon as she laid him on the ground, he started to splutter and cough water.

"You okay, Toasty?" Ember asked as she squeezed water out of her hair. She was wetter than a drowned cat. Toasty croaked in affirmation. "Okay. Okay. Okay."

In the distance, a dark, cloaked figure disappeared into the line of trees.

A chill spread through Ember's veins. Something about the dark figure appeared wrong. It must be Mallorus or one of his followers. One of them must have flooded the school to make sure everyone was distracted as they enacted their notorious plan. But what exactly were they up to?

Without thinking twice, Ember shot towards the forest, taking her talisman off as she ran.

"Ember, wait up," called a voice behind her. Ember glanced over her shoulder. Her friends were racing towards her. Her step faltered as she let them catch up to her.

Parker shot her an offended look. "Were you seriously going to leave us behind?"

"I saw someone up ahead," Ember explained. "I needed to find out who it was."

Chloe's eyes widened. "Do you think it was Mallorus?"

"Or one of his followers," Ember said grimly.

"I would like to know who flooded the school," Parker said. "This is like the second time I almost drowned in two weeks."

"Do you think it's a prank?" Chloe said, taking her video-cam out of her pocket.

"Too dangerous to be a prank," Ember said. People were quite literally being flooded out of the school and expelled on the lawn outside.

"Is your recorder okay?" Parker said.

"I'm not sure. It's not starting," Chloe said. "Maybe it got some water on it."

"Must have been a Water user, and a pretty destructive one at that," Elias said. "The question is if it was a remnant or somebody else?"

"We'll find out soon enough," Ember said. "Now, come on, into the forest before somebody sees us out here and we all get suspended."

Parker and Elias took off their respective talismans. "Even though we're not wearing it anymore, the forest still has the potential to hurt us," Elias reminded them.

Ember knew the risks, but they outweighed the urge to find the truth. "I know, so if any of you—"

"Please don't give us the cliché dialogue of who-wants-out. That's boring," Parker said.

Ember cracked a reluctant grin. "So who's in?"

There was a chorus of affirmation. Ember beamed at them. She hadn't set out to look for friends, but they had found her anyway. She took a deep breath and stared up at the looming forest. Together, the four of them entered the forest for the second time.

Chapter Twenty-Six

SHAPE-SHIFTER

The suffocating darkness surrounded them. An ominously thick layer of mist had rolled in, making it impossible to see farther than a few feet away. The forest writhed and thrummed beneath their feet, alive, but it had yet to know of their presence.

"As long as we keep quiet and don't call attention to ourselves, we'll be fine," Elias said.

The tree branches creaked above them, making Chloe jump. She clutched Parker's sleeve as they walked. Parker pulled her closer. It was pretty endearing to watch them.

"The forest is giving me the heebie-jeebies," Elias said.

"That's the entire point," Ember said, who flanked the rest. The arc of her Glo-Torch illuminated the thick foliage around them, but there was no sign of Mallorus' sigil anywhere. "Are you sure we're going in the right direction?"

"I see it," Chloe said, pointing at something in the distance, and sure enough, the iridescent glow of the sigil flickered. It was almost faded and barely even visible.

"Can you touch it?" Ember asked. Elias nodded and walked up to it before putting a tentative hand over it. He remained motionless for a few minutes while the other three held their breath. He looked up and shook his head. "I see nothing."

Ember sighed. "Let's try farther."

They walked for fifteen more minutes before they came across the next sign. This one was darker than before, as if it had been etched recently. This time Elias was braver. He didn't hesitate to put his palm over it.

His eyes had shut, and when he opened them, his irises were no longer visible.

"What the—" Ember said, gaping.

"He's having a vision," Parker said. "My mother's a clairvoyant. They look like that when they're seeing something."

Elias seemed to finally snap out of whatever trance he had been in. "I saw something," he said. "I'm not sure, I need to keep looking."

He stumbled ahead, his steps certain as if he knew exactly where he needed to go.

"What's going on?" Chloe asked.

"Let's just keep following him," Parker said. "Maybe he's found the Trace and he's leading us on the trail."

Chloe thumped her hand over the body of the video-cam. "It still won't start."

"Chloe, focus, we need to keep our eyes on Elias," Parker said.

Ember nodded and hurried over to Elias, who was moving surprisingly fast. "Yes," he said. "It's getting clearer now. I see her. She was here."

Ember's ears perked up. "See who?"

"Nadie," Elias said. It was eerie to see him like this. He didn't seem like himself anymore. He sat on the ground as if he were looking for someone. "She's in a clearing of some sort. She is scared. I see fire, or maybe just a blinding ray of light? I'm not sure."

"Why is he seeing Nadie, though?" Parker asked.

"Maybe she saw the symbol and touched it," Ember said. "The most important thing is that Elias has a way of finding her."

"Right," Parker said, his jaw gritted. He looked like he was about to say something but thought better of it.

Elias continued to weave in and out of trees until he finally disappeared behind a thick hedge of bushes.

"Elias, wait up," Chloe cried, taking off after him. Ember followed. They found themselves in a meadow of some kind. It was filled with brilliant violet wildflowers.

That was where Ember saw her. It was Nadie. She was lying on the ground in the same dress that Ember had last seen her in, and she appeared to be unconscious, her cheek turned to the dirt.

"You see that, Parker? We found her," Ember said, jogging up to Nadie. Relief crashed into Ember, which quickly turned into horror when she realized that Nadie wasn't moving.

"Nadie!" Ember called. Her hands brushed over Nadie's body, but they found no purchase, and just as quickly, the body vanished in a cloud of vapor. Ember stumbled back in surprise.

"What is this place?" she murmured under her breath. "And what was that thing?"

Elias had stopped walking. His irises were turned inside-out, and only the whites of his eyes were visible. Chloe was shaking him hard. "Elias, Elias, what is wrong with you?"

"He's not going to recover so quickly, child," said a voice. A cloaked figure stepped out of the dark. "Corrupted magic isn't everyone's forte, and I imagine especially not for a mere remnant child."

Ember pushed Chloe behind her as she faced the figure. "Who are you? Reveal yourself."

The man stepped forward. Ember squinted at him, the Glo-Torch raised above her head. "Travis Burke?" she said. It was the Zoo-Keep. "What are you doing here?"

"I thought I heard something," Travis said, circling them to stand in front of Elias. He had a look of utter fascination on his face.

Ember narrowed her eyes. Something about him seemed off. "So you came out to investigate?"

Travis fixed his onyx eyes on her, dark and pitiless. "Why else?"

"Were you the one I saw talking to my father a few weeks ago at the edge of the forest?" Ember asked as something occurred to her.

He cocked his head. "Did you now? You seem to be quite the detective, don't you?"

Something was definitely off about him.

"You know, people really underestimate the remnants, think they are capable of nothing more than bringing destruction, just as they thought of me."

A chill passed down Ember's spine, and goosebumps rose up her arms. "W-who are you?"

"I think you already know," the voice said, chuckling.

"Run," Ember said, shoving Chloe back towards the line of trees they had emerged from. She tugged on Elias's arm, who still seemed to be trapped in a trance. His body was stiff, and Ember had to grit her teeth to pull him alongside her. Above them, the sky changed rapidly. Distant thunder stuck.

Ember glanced up at the sky before turning to Elias. "Snap out of it, please."

Chloe panted as she ran. "Where's Parker?"

Ember looked around. There was no sign of him.

"He was clever enough to abandon you," said Travis from the back. The three remnants increased their pace as they darted out of the clearing, but they weren't fast enough.

A bolt of power shot through Ember, paralyzing her. She keeled over and fell face-first on the ground. Blades of grass dug into her cheek. A bolt of light shot past her, illuminating everything in its wake. It was headed right at Chloe. She screamed as the orb hit her and landed several feet away, and Elias convulsed on a bed of wildflowers.

"Elias, Chloe," Ember shouted. Ember was helpless. She couldn't decide who to go after first.

Behind them, Travis Burke's booming laugh echoed, taking over the vast meadow. "Oh, I haven't had playthings in such a long while. I had almost forgotten what it felt like."

Ember glanced back to see Travis Burke. He was balancing a plasma of brilliant blue light on his left palm. That must be the thing he had used to zap them.

In Ember's arms, Elias slowly came to his senses. He blinked rapidly. "W-where am I? What's going on?"

Ember let out a choked sigh of relief. "We thought you were…"

"Guys," Chloe said, pointing at Travis in the distance.

Elias frowned. "Wait isn't that the—"

"—Zoo-Keep," Ember finished. "Yeah, that's him."

Chloe knelt beside them. "I think something is wrong with him."

"Yeah, I figured," Ember said.

"Where's Parker?" Elias asked.

Ember swallowed. "I think he's gone."

Travis, meanwhile, stretched his hands up to the sky. "The mighty forest, you have some unwanted visitors." He sneered at the trio.

Immediately, the ground beneath them began to crack and fissure. Before Ember or the others could run, thick roots came out of the earth, wrapping itself around their arms and limbs like a constricting python. The more they struggled against it, the worse it started to feel until Ember's limbs went numb.

"Why are you doing this?" Chloe asked on the verge of tears.

"You still don't get it?" Professor Burke said. "Ah, children. Never liked them. Classmates bullied me, but I showed them what I could do. Then the Society tried to bully me." He chuckled drily. "They thought they could bind me with their stupid rules. You're not supposed to take a life-force, Mal. You can't just kill people and take their powers. It's rude." He finally looked up, and Ember saw him for what he was.

"You're Mallorus," she said, her eyes widening in terror.

Travis, a.k.a. Mallorus, smiled. "Ah, you finally get it."

Ember shook her head in confusion. "So, wait, you've been teaching here at Glofiara all this while?"

"Come on, you can do better than that," Mallorus said.

"He's a Shifter," Elias said softly. "He can shift into humans, not animals. There was never an animal. No injured Tekkow. That's why Parker never saw one."

"Aren't you the clever one?" Mallorus said as his shape began to change. He became shorter, his wiry frame just a couple of inches taller than Ember's. Dark hair slowly turned into long, snow-blond hair and an equally unkempt beard that covered his chin. "Good riddance to that ugly disguise."

Ember gaped. She had seen that man many times before—in old news clippings, a commercial to warn children about excessive usage of power. And now he was real.

"What did you do to Travis?" Chloe demanded. "And Nadie."

"Patience, my child. You'll have your answers, and as for your beloved teacher—why don't you ask her yourself?"

The three friends watched in shock and awe as a second figure emerged behind Mallorus. She stood right next to him.

"Hello, children," Nadie said, smiling at them. "I guess you finally found me."

Chapter Twenty-Seven

BETRAYED

"Nadie? Wait, you've been working with him all this time?" Ember asked. She was still reeling from the shock of the revelation. Nadie looked absolutely fine. She didn't have a single scratch on her body.

"Of course," she said. "When my master beckons, I follow him without question." She bowed to Mallorus, putting a fist to her chest and then throat.

"Now, now, there's no need for that. I don't breed sheep like the Society. People follow me because they believe in my cause," Mallorus said.

Bile rose up Ember's throat.

"You mean killing innocent people?" Elias asked.

"Only the necessary ones," Mallorus said coldly.

Nadie laughed. "I still can't believe you managed to find me. The first time I thought you drowned."

Tears pooled in Ember's eyes. All this while, Nadie had been plotting their harm.

"And then you managed to best the Gatekeeper," Nadie said, shaking her head.

Ember watched her in dismay. This wasn't the Nadie she knew.

"Of course," Mallorus said. "That vapid thing sees nothing outside his unoriginal puzzles and trinket collection. We were hoping to add the four of you to it."

"Speaking of four, where's the last one?" Nadie asked, looking around.

"He has abandoned them," Mallorus said. "Well, good for him. I would say he has the most sense out of the four of you. Coming into the forest that wants to take your life? Only someone stupid would do that."

"No," Ember said. Parker must have gone looking for help. She hoped that he found it in time.

"We came here to save Nadie," Elias said. "We just didn't know she was evil."

Nadie clucked her tongue. "You're a clever one, Elias. Why didn't you figure it out?"

Because of my stubbornness, Ember thought. The signs were there all along, but she had chosen to ignore them because she had a point to prove. And it had cost her everything. The adults were right.

"You should have stayed out of the mess when Kinnera told you to," Mallorus said. "Never liked that woman, that meddling little thing."

"I almost didn't make it into Glofiara," Nadie said, examining her finger. "But three years ago, a new position opened up at the school because the teacher who was supposed to come in fell mysteriously sick, and I was able to snag the interview. But that old hag made it almost impossible for me. Fortunately, I had her lovesick puppy of a son, Detteo, to help me."

The children stared in silence.

"Since then, my beloved Nadine has been plotting my return," Mallorus said. Nadie was looking at him with undisguised adulation.

"Nadine," Ember said as she remembered something. "Or should we call you Willow? That's your real name, isn't it?"

She laughed, but there was no mirth in it. "All glamor falls away when you're in the presence of an Ancient One. You can't really lie to a celestial being, after all. We are much too tiny for that." Nadie circled the children. "The lore of the Gatekeeper has existed for ages—the one who was punished to guard all time and banished into exile by his sister, Ethilenne. He listens to all who call to him, and one of his Gateways is right here in this forest."

"He may be the Keeper of all time, but he's a lonely man," Mallorus said.

"That's how you broke into Thanatos," Chloe said. "By tricking the Gatekeeper."

"It's said to be built by the Ancient Ones themselves," Nadie said. "So naturally, we needed one to break open the gate."

The children stood in stunned silence.

"Didn't quite figure out that bit, now, did you?" Her smile faded. "I knew that pesky Kinnera would be onto me if I went back."

"Wait, Kinnera isn't working with you?" Ember said.

Nadie laughed throatily. "Is that what you thought? Why would I ever ally myself with that miserable old witch? I had no choice but to stay here until my master fully recovered and we were joined by the rest of the loyals."

"That's why we disposed of the Zoo-Keep and I took his place instead," Mallorus said.

"What did you do to him?" Elias demanded, fighting against his restraints, but the roots curled around him viciously. He was slowly turning blue. Ember looked at Chloe, and she appeared the same. Ember's body was slowly going numb, and her vision was blurring gradually. Belatedly, she realized that the roots were cutting off their blood supply.

"But I don't get it," Chloe said, shaking her head. "You didn't disappear until after Mallorus was broken out of Thanatos. We saw you on Sunday outside the temple."

"Did you?" Nadie mused. "What you saw was merely an illusion." She stretched her palm, and a figure leaped out. It was Nadie—or at least it looked enough like her to fool anyone. "I returned once to write a false note in my diary to throw off the people who might be looking for me. My master's presence at the Menagerie made it all the more possible for us to continue the farce."

"You manipulated me," Ember said.

"No, I simply told you what you wanted to hear, little lamb. You were so desperate for love that you ate up anything that I told you. And I understand why—you finally had someone you could trust, someone who would always have your back. I know what it feels like." Nadie looked up at Mallorus as she spoke. "Getting your essence was the most crucial part of our plan, and you made it so easy."

"B-but why?" Ember's sob choked at the back of her throat. "I trusted you. I liked you."

"To frame your parents, of course. Don't take it personally," Nadie said. "While the world makes a spectacle out of their imprisonment and puts them away for good, my master will return to his rightful throne. And this time, there will be no pesky Pearsons to stop him."

Ember stared at her feet as the roots continued to writhe around her.

"But of course, she bit off more than she could chew," Mallorus said. "And it left me with this excruciating pain."

His last word was loud enough to make even Nadie flinch. "I didn't realize how an untapped remnant—" she began.

"Quiet now," Mallorus said.

Ember remembered the way Travis had walked around with the limp. Her essence had wounded him. The thought of it made her lip curl up in a smile.

"What are you smiling at?" Mallorus asked, his eyes narrowed.

"Just that even a lowly remnant's essence was enough to injure you, Mallorus, the one who claims to be the most powerful of all," Ember said.

Mallorus laughed. "Do you think I really care about that stuff?"

Ember's smirk faded. Now she was confused. She had meant to antagonize him, but he seemed to be terrifyingly calm.

"You'll never be as powerful as a full-fledged magi. You know why? Because your powers will destroy you." But then the expression on his face changed. It became eerie as he stepped closer, close enough to touch them. "Don't you get it? Society isn't afraid of you because you're useless or broken, it's afraid because of what you can do. By sending you to Glofiara, by making sure you suppress your powers and that you're cast out of the community as soon as acceptable, they're protecting themselves."

Where are you, Parker? Ember thought to herself. *We need you.*

"But I've seen your potential. I see what you're capable of. Society will never accept you. It will shun you as it shuns anybody who is different, but you can join me and find your place in the world," Mallorus said. "In fact, Nadie might be able to help you make that decision. After all, she used to be like one of you."

She stepped forward, staring at Ember. "I was lying when I told you there was no way to stabilize your powers. There is a way: the Darkness."

"But doesn't it come at a cost?" Ember said softly.

"Perhaps, but it's outweighed by everything else it gives you," Nadie said.

A stunned silence followed, broken only by the ruffle of the wind caught on the trees around them.

"Never," Elias snarled. "We'll never join you."

"I was just like you, pathetic and confused, when the Dark gave me its home," Nadie said. "It gave me power and respect. Taking a life in exchange seems like a small sacrifice to make. Better to be on the winning side than the losing one."

"Ether gives us everything we need," Ember said.

"That's not going to work out for you much longer when magic as you know it runs out, when ether no longer has a hold on you," Mallorus said.

"You're bluffing," Ember said. "That'll never happen."

"It already has started. Haven't you noticed how many remnants and non-magics there are now in our community? That number will exponentially grow as magic gets out of control until Ethilenne's magic is replaced by Chaos," Mallorus said.

"You're a liar," Ember said.

"Careful, girl. I've shown restraint so far, but it will not last long if you continue to step on my patience."

He leaned in to Chloe, taking a long sniff of her while she cowered. He put his finger on her chin and tilted it up so Chloe had no choice but to look at him. "Ah, this one looks familiar for some reason. She might not seem like much, but she will have her usefulness."

"Let go of her," Ember growled.

"Ah, the power of friendship," Mallorus said. "Can't say I had much of it when I was a kid."

A movement at the back of the clearing caught Ember's attention. It was a small ripple, a tear in the blanket of darkness. She squinted at it to figure out what it was when Mallorus eyed her suspiciously. Ember tried to relax her expression.

"I can hear her heartbeat quicken," Nadie said, whipping to the back. "The fourth one never left."

Mallorus laughed. "I forgot how stupid children can be sometimes, too driven by emotions."

"Come out, Parker," Nadie said, walking up to Chloe. "Or I kill her right now."

"Nadie, no," Ember said desperately as Nadie raised Chloe's chin as if she were about to strike her.

"You wouldn't do that," came a voice. "Leave her alone." Parker emerged in open sight.

Mallorus shot him with one of his blazing lightning streaks, and Parker fell to the ground in a heap. "I've changed my mind. I'll kill this one."

"NO!" Ember screamed, her voice almost guttural as she fought against her restraints harder than ever. The vines gripped her viciously. The temperature of her body shot up until it felt like she was sitting on the lap of the sun. "Don't hurt him."

Mallorus chuckled. "What are you going to do about it? You're at my mercy, child."

The voices in Ember's head that had been begging her for release since the day of her test of age grew louder and louder until she didn't hear anything else over the roar of it.

The forest fell away, and she was back at the Society headquarters, her palms clammy with sweat as she waited her turn.

"It's going to be okay," Dad was saying. Back then, Ember thought he was trying to reassure her, but he already knew the outcome. He already knew what she was. He just had to play along.

"You're going to be fine, baby," Rosetta said, squeezing Ember's shoulder. "No matter what the outcome of today's test, you'll always be my little Em."

They both knew the truth.

Ember nodded as she stepped through the door. The girl before her came out in tears. Ember recognized the blond hair now. It was Clarisse. It was clear that she had failed her test. She looked up and glared at Ember as if that were somehow her fault.

Ember took a deep breath and left her parents behind to step through the door.

Three people wearing maroon mantles sat in front of her. Their gazes were glazed with boredom.

"Class and subclass, please?" one of them said.

"Elemental—fire," Ember replied, the word coming out on a shaky note.

"Okay, let us begin with the test of demonstration," said one of the panel members. "Start a concentrated source of fire."

Ember took a deep breath, knowing that she would have to focus her entire energy to ignite the flame. Unlike the rest of her family, her magic rarely listened to her, coming out in chaotic bursts. But she had been practicing.

Ember squinted at her palm as she attempted to draw out a fire. Nothing happened. Sweat poured down her back as seconds ticked. She was aware of the panel members slowly losing their patience.

"Are you having trouble, child?" one of them asked.

She shook her head and gritted her teeth.

"Come on," she breathed. "Come on, listen to me."

Fire sprang to life on her arms—more than she had expected. It engulfed her, but it didn't burn her. Her magic was her own.

"That's it," she said. Dad had told her that most of the would-be remnants had trouble passing the first stage itself. Their magic was too chaotic to impress the panel members, but Ember had passed it with flying colors, which meant that she still had a shot. She would have to pass the other two tests to qualify, but so far, it looked good.

The panel members nodded as they scribbled something on their sheets.

"Now, for the test of limit," said the dark, curly-haired woman. Immediately following her words, a low hum filled the air. The platform she was standing on began to change. Three wooden rungs appeared from the bottom, each of increasing height. Each one of them had an effigy of a straw doll.

"Use a concentrated ball of your elemental magic to hit and knock each one to the floor."

This was tricky. Were they making it especially hard for her?

"What if I burn it?" Ember asked.

"It's fine, but make sure that your aim doesn't stray. Let your elemental guide you," said a taller, mustached man. "It shouldn't be a problem if you're not a remnant."

Remnant—the word made her nervous. At age ten, her sister was wielding her powers with her eyes closed. She was born to be a witch and, in the future, a powerful sorcerer even. Ember had to give her best.

She tried to summon a ball of fire, but it fizzled out in her palm like a match-stick. She tried again and again, and after five minutes or so, the ball of fire roared to life. She aimed it at the first doll, hitting its feet instead of the body. But it did the trick and fell to the ground. She tried the next one, but this time, no matter how Ember tried, she failed to summon fire. Seconds trickled into minutes, but nothing came out. Her ether had fizzled away for good.

"You can go," one of the panel members said. Realization sank into her. She had failed her test. Desperation clawed its way into her chest. She couldn't lose; she couldn't bear to see the disappointment in her parents' faces when they found out what she really was.

"Please," Ember said. "Give me another chance. I can do it."

"I think it's time for lunch. Tea or coffee?" They talked amongst themselves, Ember long forgotten. Her vision blurred as she sank to the floor on her palms, defeated. Her fate was sealed for good.

An odd feeling raced through her heart, making her feverish. Her head throbbed as if someone were banging it from behind to let it out. Ember tried to breathe, but it was becoming harder and harder. Her eyes closed, and she didn't even notice when fire trickled out of her hand. The wooden floor caught fire easily. All it needed was a spark.

By the time the panel members noticed, the platform was on fire with Ember still inside the heart of its ring. Mallorus was right. Ember had

Chaos within herself, Chaos that she had tried to keep away, but it was time to unleash it.

The dam inside Ember that she had been holding in—her grief and her shame that she had hidden away—finally burst through. This time, though, she was in the forest.

Nadie shot a confused look at Mallorus. "What is happening?"

Mallorus' hold on Parker loosened as he watched Ember, who had turned her restraints to cinders. She sank to the floor, and as she did, fire snaked out of her arms and followed a trail through the grass, scorching everything in its wake. The ring of fire spread fast, engulfing them in a matter of minutes.

Parker, who had managed to escape Mallorus, made his way to Elias to cut through his restraints before moving on to Chloe.

"What's going on?" Nadie said, staring at Ember, who was still on the ground, an odd shimmer around her body, like the bluest part of the flame before it grew stronger. "She's pure fire."

Suddenly, there were voices in the distance. "Is anybody there?"

"Let's go," Mallorus said. "We need to get out of here."

"But she—"

"Nadine," Mallorus said. Nadie walked to his side just as the thick wall of fire cut them off from the four remnants. The smoke was so thick at this point that they began to cough as it penetrated their lungs. Ember's eyes watered as she finally came back to her senses.

"W-what?" she said, sounding disoriented.

Elias clutched her shoulders. "You okay?"

"I'm fine, but the fire..." Ember started. Elias' face was illuminated by the red-orangish glow of the flames. "I started it."

"Yes, you did," he said.

Ember sucked in a breath. It was just like when she had almost burned the testing hall at the Society. "I don't—"

She was cut off by voices.

"Someone's here to look for us," Chloe said.

Parker waved his arms. "We're here. Over here."

Moments later, a strong gust of wind blew at them, almost ripping them off the ground. When the tornado passed, the fire had reduced to cinders. As the thick smoke cleared, two figures came into view. At first, Ember thought it was Mallorus and Nadie. But moments later, Professor Detteo and Summer were making their way to them.

"Oh my Ethilenne," Summer said, running up to her. "Are you okay?"

They were covered in soot but looked otherwise unharmed. Toasty the toad made a dramatic entrance as he hopped on top of Ember's head. Even he had escaped the fire unscathed.

Summer noted the thick, red welts on her sister's arm and brushed her fingers over it. "What happened to you?"

"The forest," Ember said. "It attacked us."

"As did Mallorus," Elias said.

Summer's eyes widened. "He was here?"

"He has been here all this while," Parker said.

"That's ridiculous, we would have known if the forest were breached," Professor Detteo said. He stopped as if he could sense something. "Well, until now anyway."

"That's because they never left, and technically Nadie used the forest to rescue him from his prison," Ember said, a sinking feeling in her chest. They were gone. That wasn't part of the plan.

"Wait, what are you talking about?" Professor Detteo said, frowning. "Nadie would never do that."

"I wouldn't put it past her," said a voice from behind. Headmistress Kinnera was walking towards them. "Ever since I recognized Nadine as a former student, I have been keeping an eye on her."

Parker's eyes widened. "Wait, you knew about her?"

"I never forget a face," Headmistress Kinnera said.

"Why would she go to school at Glofiara?" Summer said.

"Because she's a—well, she was a remnant," Ember said. "Until Mallorus changed her." Ember turned toward the headmistress. "Is that why you told me to stay away from her?" she asked.

"I had my suspicions. Remnants don't simply become warlocks. But I never imagined she was one of Mallorus' followers," the headmistress said, shaking her head.

"She helped Mallorus escape and now they're both gone," Parker said.

"Nobody is going to believe you without proof," said Professor Detteo.

"Actually," Chloe, who had been silent till now, spoke up. "We have proof." She held up the video-recorder so that the others could see. The footage was scratchy in places, but it showed both Mallorus and Nadie in multiple frames. It was clear enough that there would be no mistake who Mallorus really was.

Headmistress Kinnera took a step back. "So it's true then. He *is* back."

"I told you there was something about Nadie's disappearance that seemed off," Ember said. The headmistress fell silent before walking away.

Summer stared at her. "What's wrong with her?"

"My mother has traumatic memories attached to Mallorus," Professor Detteo explained. "She worked with the Pearsons when they were trying to bring him down, and she...well, Mallorus took away my father and tortured him for weeks before his body was found."

Ember clapped a hand over her mouth. "Oh no."

"Yeah," Professor Detteo said. "But it's not the time to delve into the past. Let's get you out of here before—" He paused. "You took your talismans off."

"We figured out what they really did," Elias said.

Ember expected Detteo to reprimand them, but he simply nodded. "Come on, the school is already in upheaval. Somebody flooded the building. Only the library was unscathed. You guys wouldn't by any chance have anything to do with it, now, would you?"

The children glanced at each other. "No, of course not." Until now, Ember was under the belief that Professor Detteo was the one planning the attacks. But if Mallorus had hurt his father, why would he do that? Things didn't add up.

Summer and Detteo led the four children out of the forest. Ember's Glo-Torch had been destroyed sometime after they confronted Mallorus. Chloe was huddled up between Elias and Parker as if they were her sentries.

"Something happened to you," Elias said to Ember. "It's like you lost control."

"I could say the same for you," she pointed out.

Elias rubbed his head. "I didn't lose control. It was like something temporarily took control over me, as if I knew where to go."

Ember smirked. "Right."

"Do you think it was because of the dark symbols?" Chloe said.

Elias shuddered. "I don't ever want to find out."

Parker's gaze remained on Ember. "Is this what happened to you at the Society, during the test of age? Is this what Clarisse was threatening you with?"

Ember nodded, hugging Toasty to her chest. She was grateful that they had faced Mallorus and lived to tell the tale. "I thought my parents had buried it for good, but apparently not."

"But Ember," Parker said. "You don't have to be ashamed. You were incredibly powerful back there."

"It doesn't matter," she said, shaking her head. "At the end of the day, I still failed the test."

"You know, I never understood how four people and some arbitrary test can define us for the rest of our lives," Parker said. "It seems incredibly unfair."

"No wonder the Misveez fought back," said Elias.

"The Misveez?" Ember said, remembering how the headmistress had called her that.

"Yeah, they're an underground organization by the former Glofiara students who believe that the segregation between remnants and full-fledged magic users is an obsolete concept, and how unfair it is," Elias said. "They disbanded a few years ago."

This was news to Ember. She didn't have much time to think about it, however, as they emerged from the forest. The school grounds were still teeming with people. They crowded around the four friends, asking questions.

Summer and Xander ushered them through before dropping them at their respective dorms. By the time they returned, the mini-flood was gone and the teachers were helping restore the dorm rooms to their usual condition. Ember's clothes were drenched but that was the worst part of it. "Rest up," Summer said. "You have a long day ahead."

Ember nodded at her sister and turned to walk up the stairs when Summer said from behind, "I'm glad you're okay."

Chapter Twenty-Eight

THE GOLDEN INVITATION

By the following day, rumors of all sorts were swirling around the campus. Many said that the four students had thwarted Mallorus's evil attempt to hijack Glofiara and take all the students hostage. Somehow they learned that he had been disguised as Travis Burke all this while.

"When I met him last week, he wanted me to follow him into the forest," a boy called Joseph was saying. "I should have known that something was up."

"Yeah, he was acting really fishy during one of the classes," said a second-year student. "I totally knew that it was Mallorus. He seemed evil."

Travis's body was never found, but it was assumed that Mallorus had probably taken his life-force for his transformation.

By the next morning, two Society members had shown up to interrogate Ember and her friends. They asked questions for several hours. All four cooperated with them, while the rest of the story was filled in by Chloe's trusty video-cam.

The tall one shook his head. "I can't believe it; he's really back. What happens now?"

The agents left with a promise to follow up with them soon. Before the children were excused, however, one of them looked at Ember and said, "You'll be pleased to know that your parents' trial has been put on hold until the Society investigates these claims."

"It's a good thing you had that non-magic device with you, Chloe," Parker said.

Chloe grinned. "I told you we sort are quite handy."

"And reliable," Elias said, ruffling her hair fondly. His smile faded. "Sometimes I feel like my abilities are more of a curse."

"Yeah," Ember said, looking down at her hands. "I feel that." If Detteo hadn't been there to stop the fire, who knows what would have happened? It could have spread into a wildfire, or worse, made it all the way to Glofiara. She shuddered at the thought.

"But it's behind us now," Parker said. "We did what needed to be done. We exposed Mallorus. The Society will take care of him."

Ember nodded. She hoped that Parker was right.

Meanwhile, a lot seemed to have changed at Glofiara. People who had been shunning Ember just a week ago lined up to have a conversation. Even Chloe was gaining attention. They would come up to her with silly little questions and ask her to recount the details of their forest adventure. That was her favorite part. So far, Ember had heard about four-hundred-fifty-seven variations, and it all began with how brave they had been and how scared Mallorus was to make an escape.

Clarisse was the only one who seemed to be unhappy at the attention the four misfits were getting. "I mean, it's not even a big deal," she said during their Facing History class.

"Can you go up to Mallorus and come back unscathed?" Elias challenged. "I would like to see you try."

"Yeah, try being mean to him," Chloe suggested. "Maybe that will help."

Clarisse's face reddened as she stomped away. Ember stifled a laugh, but at the back of her mind, she couldn't help but wonder about the person who had flooded the school. Despite Headmistress Kinnera's best attempts, the culprit was never found. Ember couldn't shake the feeling that it had something to do with Mallorus and Nadie.

They were still on the run, and the last they were seen was in Bangladesh, and after that they seemed to drop off the map entirely. Mallorus was probably still recuperating. Ember shuddered to think about what would happen when he finally regained his former strength. But that was a matter the adults could deal with.

A week later, the children received a golden envelope with an invitation inside. Their presence was requested at the Conservation Society headquarters.

A para-copter came to pick them up from Glofiara. The four children bid goodbye to their classmates as they each slid into a leather seat. The pilot waited until they had buckled themselves in before propelling forward and shooting off the ground.

"Where do you think we are headed?" Ember asked. The Society headquarters never remained in the same place for long. Sometimes it could be found in the depths of an ocean, on top of a mountain, or even in the sky.

Elias, who was wearing a formal jacket, fidgeted with the tie around his neck. "No clue. I think it's the same place as last time."

"Probably," Parker said. "It's been barely six months since we got tested."

"How time flies," Chloe said, her cheeks pressed against the glass. "And now we're flying."

Ember peered down and felt a lurch in her stomach. She didn't care much for heights. She could no longer see the school or even the forest. It looked like miles and miles of empty, barren lands as the charm around it had come into place again.

They flew for an hour or so until the para-copter finally began to descend. The four watched in fascination as they landed on a small island in front of a rather unremarkable building. But that wasn't what distracted Ember. It was the swarm of reporters crowded on the ground outside. She could spot the representative vehicle for EtherTV even from up in the sky, and they didn't look like the only news channel there.

"We are famous," Elias said, his face full of wide-eyed awe. "I can't believe this."

"Neither can I," Chloe echoed.

As soon as the para-copter landed, the reporters rushed to them, their mics shoving up at their faces. "Tell us about Mallorus. How did you encounter him? How did you escape?"

"We didn't run away, he did," Elias said, his tone smug.

Ember began to walk away when she was cornered by at least twenty reporters. "Miss Pearson, how do you feel about the fact that the Pearson trial has been dropped?"

"They're heroes, always were and always will be," Ember said. "And I think they should have been given more credit instead of being thrown under the bus at the first instant."

She expected the reporters to back off, but they pounced on her like hungry crocodiles. "Did you seek Mallorus out on your own? Did you want to prove your parents' innocence? Are you and Mr. Kamali dating?"

Ember was caught off-guard by the last question. "Excuse me? I am just thirteen," Ember said. What was wrong with these people?

"Leave her be," said a voice right behind the reporters. The crowd parted to let a tall, bearded man in. His silvery-white beard was beaded, and he wore the familiar white mantle of a Society member. Ember swore that she had seen him somewhere before but couldn't place him.

"Welcome, Miss Pearson, please follow me inside. And I advise you and your friends not to speak to any of the reporters," the man said.

"Well, it's already too late for that," Ember said, peering at Parker and Elias, who were practically preening themselves like peacocks as the cameras took picture after picture. "Who invited them anyway?"

"Anything related to Mallorus is treated as a sensation. Good or bad, he's one of the most powerful of us," the man said.

"And you are?"

"Shefikaya Renous," he replied.

"Oh, Ember," said someone nearby. Ember's parents walked towards her. She ran up to them, promptly engulfing them in a bear hug. Tears streamed down her face as her dad picked her up and swung her around just like he used to when she was five.

"I can't believe you're safe," Ember said.

Her parents peered at her with identical smiles. "We wouldn't be if it weren't for you, sweet-pea," Rosetta Pearson said before her face darkened. "Tell me the truth, Em. Did you seek him out on your own?"

"I had no choice," Ember said, shuffling her feet. "I tried to warn the adults, but they wouldn't listen to me."

"We didn't want any trouble for you," Rosetta said. "That's why we kept you away."

Ember turned to her father. "Back at Glofiara, you suspected Travis, right?"

George Pearson looked surprised. "I have known Travis for a few years now, and we have worked on some cases together, and I felt there was something off about him, but how did you...?"

"I saw you in the forest," Ember said.

"Ethilenne forgive me," George said. "I knew something was wrong. I should have done something about it."

"You couldn't have figured it out," Ember said. "Or maybe you did and Mallorus made you forget. He can mess with anybody's head."

Her parents nodded. "Unfortunately, we know that all too well. But you...you and your friends managed to figure out the truth, Em."

"Our children are smart and intuitive," Shefikaya said, walking up to them. "We just don't give them as much credit."

"We are grateful to our Ember," George said, hugging her again. "We wouldn't be here if it weren't for her."

Shefikaya cleared his throat in embarrassment. "On behalf of the Society, I would like to formally apologize to you."

Ember's father nodded. "We have no ill feelings for the Society. We have served it for years and will continue to do so for all the years to come."

"I'm glad that we still have your loyalty," Shefikaya said with a nod.

Around Ember, the other children were being reunited with their families too. Elias' parents were dressed in similar stiff-gray clothes like him. All three of them wore glasses. Ember understood where Elias had gotten his unusual streaks from.

Parker had been reunited with his mother, who wore a red mantle with the Society's crest sewed into it. Chloe was the only one left alone. Ember beckoned her to come closer. She looked up at George and Rosetta Pearson shyly as Ember introduced her to them. "My foster parents were invited, but they couldn't make it," Chloe said.

"You're family now, dear," Rosetta said, touching her chin fondly. "Thank you for having my Ember's back. She couldn't have done it without her friends."

"We're all going to stay here for a week," Shefikaya said.

"A week?" Ember said, raising her brows.

"Well, yeah, we need to make a statement about Mallorus, give people assurance that they have nothing to worry about."

Ember hesitated. "Would that be the right thing to do?"

"Of course," Shefikaya said. "We don't want people to panic. That would make matters worse."

"Right," Ember said.

"Now come on," Shefikaya said, ushering her towards the steps to the building where the rest of the children had gathered. "Big smiles, everyone. Big smiles."

The four of them stood side by side as picture after picture were taken.

"Now one of the Pearson family, please," a reporter called out. Loud jeers followed.

Parker, Elias, and Chloe were replaced by Rosetta and George Pearson who each put a hand on her shoulder as they clicked pictures. After they were done, they called out for single shots of Ember. She was smiling so much that by the end of the photo session, her cheeks hurt. None of the other three were being called for a solo profile, which Ember found odd.

They entered the tall, sprawling hallway of the Society building, leaving the din of the crowd outside. A familiar spark of unease sparked in her belly as Ember remembered what had transpired the last time she was here.

Shefikaya walked alongside her. "You know, Ember, I watched the footage of you in the forest. It seems like we made a mistake with you." The man walked away abruptly, leaving Ember to gape. What could he possibly mean by that?

Ember followed Chloe up the stairs to the grand auditorium, where they had been invited to get their medal of valor. It had been two days since they had landed at the island, and Ember felt like, in the whirlwind of dress fittings and long speeches, she barely had any time to talk to her friends. The news that had followed since had made her uneasy as well. It was all about how Ember and her friends had defeated Mallorus, almost as if he were gone for good.

"Are you sure about this?" Ember asked.

"It was Parker's idea. He found an unused attic," Chloe replied. "Em, it's too dark here. Can you please—"

Ember hesitated, but just for a second. Ever since their encounter in the forest with Mallorus and Nadie, she had been careful to use her magic sparingly. She flicked her fingers, and a small flame came to life. The old Ember—the one who had arrived fresh-faced at Glofiara—would have been thrilled to do it. But the present one knew the cost of her power. She wasn't the only one who had changed. There were subtle changes in all three of her friends. They had grown up, in a way. Even Parker, who usually cracked jokes, was sober.

They finally came up to a landing. Parker appeared at the mouth of the attic and helped the two girls up.

"How did you even discover this place?" Ember asked, looking around the sparingly lit place with a slanted wooden ceiling.

"My mother works here, remember?" Parker said.

"That's right," Ember said. She had yet to talk to her, but she had seen her outside.

"I used to come to visit with her when I was younger."

"Are you guys overwhelmed?" Elias asked. "I mean, don't get me wrong, I love being in the spotlight—"

He was interrupted by Parker snorting. "Who would have thought?"

"I totally get what you're saying," Chloe said. "Sometimes it's too overwhelming."

Laughter from the ballroom downstairs trickled up to the attic. Ember couldn't believe that they were having premature celebrations, especially in the face of everything they had seen. Mallorus had incredible powers, and if Ember had to guess, his time in isolation had only made him stronger, giving him time to recuperate.

"And they're out there pretending as if Mallorus has lost when he's just getting started," Ember said. Their ignorance made Ember angry. The Conservation Society had been quick to blame her parents, and now they were saving face by pretending the problem didn't exist anymore.

"Do you think he was telling the truth about the Darkness curing the remnants?" Parker asked.

Ember shrugged. "I don't know. But what I do know is that our troubles haven't ended yet. Remember what the Gatekeeper told us."

"It's only the beginning," Elias muttered darkly under his breath. And so it was.

Dear Reader,

Hello there! Did you enjoy our story story story?

If you want to join the misfits as we go on more adventures, then leave a review review review!

Otherwise, we won't know if you're up for the next one one one. And when we get sucked into more magic school drama, you may never hear about it it it!

You can leave a review wherever you found the book book book.

I'm excited to see you for the next mystery adventure adventure adventure!

Fingers crossed there are tasty snacks snacks snacks...

Yours Truly,
Toasty the Toad (and Ember)

Misfit Magic School Character Cards

Get to know your favorite misfits better with their character cards!

Download the cards for FREE:

marinajbowman.com/mms-charactercards

ABOUT THE AUTHOR

MARINA J. BOWMAN is a writer and explorer who travels the world searching for wildly fantastical stories to share with her readers. Ever since she was a child, she has been fascinated with uncovering long lost secrets and chasing the mythical, magical, and supernatural.

Marina enjoys sailing, flying, and nearly all other forms of transportation. She never strays far from the ocean for long, as it brings her both inspiration and peace. She stays away from the spotlight to maintain privacy and ensure the more unpleasant secrets she uncovers don't catch up with her.

As a matter of survival, Marina nearly always communicates with the public through her representative, Devin Cowick. Ms. Cowick is an entrepreneur who shares Marina's passion for travel and creative storytelling and is the co-founder of Code Pineapple.

Other book series by Marina J. Bowman include SCAREDY BAT, a vampire detective series, and THE LEGEND OF PINEAPPLE COVE, a mythical island adventure series.

Made in the USA
Monee, IL
26 January 2023

26293332R00142